About the author

Dawud Wharnsby (b. 1972) first b   g
music and performing while in hi   er
began in 1995 and has yielded ove   ie
internationally-popular albums *T..*   *ut
Seeing the Fields*. Dawud has been a pioneer in the development of
English-language spiritual hymns (*nashid*) inspired by Qur'anic
teachings. As a voice for socially-conscious and spiritually-minded
believers in the twenty-first century, his work has inspired a
generation of educators, artists, poets and musicians. Dawud
performs worldwide and frequently lectures at schools, conferences
and universities. Dawud and his family reside seasonally between
their homes in Pakistan, Canada and the United States.

Select Recordings

Off to Reap the Corn (with Heather Chappell)	1993
Fine Flowers in the Valley (with Heather Chappell)	1994
Blue Walls and the Big Sky	1995
A Whisper of Peace	1996
Colours of Islam	1997
Road to Madinah	1998
The Letter – Songs of Struggle and Hope	1999
Sunshine, Dust and the Messenger	2000
The Prophet's Hands	2002
A Different Drum	2005
The Poets and the Prophet (with Bill Kocher)	2006
Out Seeing the Fields (featuring Idris Phillips)	2007

Books

Field Tromping	1993
Dawud Wharnsby – Nasheed Artist	2005

FOR WHOM THE TROUBADOUR SINGS

FOR WHOM THE TROUBADOUR SINGS

COLLECTED POETRY AND SONGS

DAWUD WHARNSBY

KUBE
PUBLISHING

First published by Kube Publishing Ltd,
Markfield Conference Centre
Ratby Lane, Markfield,
Leicestershire LE67 9SY
United Kingdom
Tel: +44 (0) 1530 249230
Fax: +44 (0) 1530 249656
Website: www.kubepublishing.com
Email: info@kubepublishing.com

Poems, prose and song lyrics are all
published with the permission of the author.

A Catalogue-in-Publication Data record for
this book is available from the British Library.

ISBN 978-1-84774-011-3 *paperback*

Typeset by: Nasir Cadir
Cover Design: Inspiral Design

To Maryam,
welcome to this world.
Take care of it,
and it will take care of you.

Contents

Part II: To Inspire

PART III: TO REMIND

PART IV: FOR THE FAITHFUL

Part V: For the King's Court

PART I

SONGS OF THE JOURNEY

White Moon

White moon in a blue sky,
across from a red eye,
sinking fast as day goes past
and night will quietly lie.

White moon in a black sky,
across from a red eye,
rising fast as night goes past
and children rub their waking eyes.

Little Boy

Little boy,
locked out of your house,
how will you get inside?
The handle is too high.
You've stood on the stoop
to reach and push and try.

There's someone there you know –
but they don't hear your call.
Maybe they'll forget,
and you'll never get in again?

Little boy,
locked out of your house,
how will you get inside?
The handle is too high.
You've stood on the stoop,
to reach and push and cry.

Secret Friend

It is warm.
I like the sun.
Won't you get your bicycle?
We can have a race.
We will ride away.
Come to my yard,
I've a swing there.
We can swing and I will push you.
You can push me too.
We will fly all day.
We can fly away.

There's a box,
in my garage,
we can paint it up real fancy.
It will be our fort,
for a secret club to meet.
My dog's nice,
and he's so strong.
Let's tie him to my wooden wagon.
You say 'Mush' and he
can pull us down the street.

Do you like hot dogs for supper?
I don't think I like them either.
Not the wiener,
just the bun.
We like rain,
best with thunder.
It used to make us cry before,
but now,
we think it's fun.

All those kids,
who yell those bad words,
make me mad.
I want to hit them.
But you and I,
will run away.
You don't laugh
at my new glasses.
You think Secord is a nice name.
I'm glad
I met you today.

My Mom gets mad,
when I say,
that you are my very best friend.
She tells me,
not to lie.
Boy, I wish
that she could meet you,
but she says that she can't see you.
Very strange.
I don't know why.

You know what?
I think you're cool.
You make me laugh,
I really like you.
Sleep at my house,
foreverynight.
What to hear
a secret Friend?
Sometimes I still cry when there's thunder.
Always hold my hand tight.

Boy, I wish
my Mom would meet you,
but she says that she can't see you.
Very strange.
I don't know why.
Very strange.
And I don't lie.
Always hold my hand tight.
Friend.

Antisocialsong

You've asked if I'm OK eleven times now.
I've told you I feel fine.
Yes, I like the table you've chosen.
Yes, I'm having a good time.
No, I don't want a sip of your beer.
No, the music is not too loud.
Yes, I'm happy to be sitting here,
I just like to watch the crowd.

> You could call me antisocial,
> I've called myself that sometimes too,
> but I just prefer to be alone,
> and that's nothing against you.

You could call and there's no answer,
chances are I'm not home.
You could call and there's no answer,
chances are I'm just not answering my phone.

> You could call me antisocial,
> I've called myself that a time or two,
> but I just prefer to be alone,
> and that's nothing against you.

Today's a sweet day to get away.
Perhaps I might go for a walk.
I can hear those corn fields calling me.
Funny, but I didn't think a corn field could talk.
I don't think that I will bathe today,
I think I smell alright to me.
I think I'll find a forest and take off all my clothes
and lie down naked in the leaves.

You could call me antisocial,
I've called myself that a time or two,
but I just prefer to be alone,
and that's nothing against you.

Assess Your Life

Sit down, assess your life.
You say you want to experience everything.
But you have made your choice –
you have left now you must stay away.
Where is your logic, can't you see that you cannot do everything?
Your art and morals drip away.
Try to catch them if you can.
You can't.

Change the world with your coffee and your cup,
from the café where you sit and philosophize.
Your little friends won't help you when your time is up,
but you can call me if need be,
and I'll try not to act surprised.

She loosens up your mind but she straps your morals down,
face it – you don't know who she is
and you'll wake up next to her and find I'm right.
Don't be offended, but I don't think you know who you are either
     anymore.
I wish you'd hurry back I miss you.
It's been so long, since where we were before.

> Save the world with your coffee and your cup,
> from the café where you sit and theorize.
> Your little friends won't help you when your time is up,
> but you can call me if need be, and I'll try not to
> act surprised.

And we're sick of this trap.
And we're sick of this crap.
And I miss you.
And you miss you too.

> Screw the world with a bottle and a smoke,
> from the hardwood floor where you lay and rub your eyes.
> Those pseudo artists, they are really quite a joke.
> So we'll both sit and laugh a while,
> 'cause we're really not surprised.

I Just Wanna Sing

Don't be surprised, don't rub your eyes,
if your confused about what you see,
in a smokey cafe that you happen in one day,
when suddenly you stumble upon me.
I'll be singin' lazy jazz or the truest of the blues,
with a band of maybe two or three.
There won't be no admission fee, no label will commission me,
'cause music faith and knowledge should be free.

I just wanna sing,
I've never known why, I just always did.
I've just sort of always had a song, since I was a kid.
I cannot understand it and I never really planned it.
How could somethin' so sweet and so good
leave a simple singin' man like me,
misunderstood?

If your car breaks down near a forgotten little town,
like Rawalpindi, Timbuktu, Brigadoon –
you'll be in for quite a stun, when you find that I'm the one,
serving burgers at the local greasy spoon.
I'll be content while I'm workin', fryin' fries and soda jerkin',
scoopin' ice cream, taking orders for tea.
'Cause I'll be singin' with each order I'll be bringin',
I'll be ketchup stained and care free.

I just wanna sing,
I've never known why, I just always did.
I've just sort of always had a song, since I was a kid.
I cannot understand it and I never really planned it.
How could somethin' so sweet and so good
leave a simple singin' man like me,
misunderstood?

Put some songs on a CD,
with the hope that other people'd wanna sing along with me.
Producers came...the price of fame...
changed my life and stole my name...
Agents and friends with personal gain.
People goin' crazy, drivin' me insane.

'Where's the next show?', 'Why don't you make a video?',
'Put on these beads and clothes and the bling, bling!'
Well, if that's all it's about than I think that I want out,
of a career that won't just let me sing.

So if you're ever all alone, in the mountains far from home,
humming as you hike so quietly,
don't be overcome with shock or lose your footing off your rocker
if you hear a distant harmony.
I'll be a hermit in those trees farming charming honey bees,
having left the music business willfully.
Songs will be my life – I'll raise a family with my wife,
'cause music faith and knowledge should be free.

> I just wanna sing,
> I've never known why, I just always did.
> I've just sort of always had a song, since I was a kid.
> I cannot understand it and I never really planned it.
> How could somethin' so sweet and so good
> leave a simple singin' man like me,
> misunderstood?

Education and the Working Man

A boatman came down walking,
his hair was dry and blown.
He bit upon his pipe
and pulled his coat closed across his chest.
Through the empty laneway,
the market had grown thinner.
The days were growing shorter,
the man knew that he was old now.
The wind from off the east,
should never chill a sailor.
The days should never run
like an everlasting Sunday.
Perhaps if he was younger,
he'd be out on the water.
But drunken at a table,
young men wish that they were older.

Boats tied up to shore.
Men tied up to shore.

There're children sleeping upstairs,
a woman on the sofa.
The ceiling looks like heaven,
his bottle is almost full yet.
To dump it or to drink it,
those are the crucial questions.
He cannot hold a job,
so he will try to hold his liquor.
He's been told he's a man,
but he feels just like a child again,
and how can you explain that
to a learning adolescent,
who's too young yet to understand,
but growing to confusion?
He may grow up to think like him...
God help him when he's grown.

Boats tied up to shore.
Men tied up to shore.

We do what they say,   (Do what you want you will anyway.)
not as they do.   (Say what you will.)
Now we have hours,
minutes, days and years to kill.

Eating education,
is like eating Christmas pudding:
too much can make your stomach sore,
too much can spoil your whole Christmas.
Learning from a man,
who learned all he learned from another,
can lead you to a safe place,
but destroy your sense of wonder.
Trapped inside a book,
locked inside a lecture,
when do you find the time to love
and spend your days in forests?
When ideals are fleeting
tell me, then who do you turn to?
They proved to you that God was dead,
and to them you're just a number.

Boats tied up to shore.
Men tied up to shore.

Afraid to Read

How many words she's read before,
she's consumed two thousand books or more.
Musty pulp and glue soundproof her tiny room.
She cannot understand why this book in her hand,
fascinates her now so much that she's almost shy to touch.
'Don't think about the words it's just a book – paper and ink'.
She reaffirms, reminds herself, 'a book can't dictate what to think.'
It invites, intrigues her more than others on her shelf.
'Is it just another book?' – she sits questioning herself.

Oh Allah,
she's so afraid to read,
the wisdom that's revealed may burrow in her mind.
She'll be obliged to admit,
she'll be obliged to submit,
but will she be strong enough to live the truth she finds?
Oh Allah,
she's so afraid to read.

The hall light is always on, every night that he is gone.
He hears his mother toss in bed, when he slips in at dawn.
In the book case by the stair, he can see it sitting there,
like a waiting, watchful, wise-man scolding him with care.
In the morning will they fight about him being out all night?
Will he resent their gift of love and not admit that they are right?
All he wants is to fit in some place,
but must he compromise his faith?
He cannot look himself or his parents in the face.
He takes the book upstairs unread and sets it closed next to his
    head,
then counts the prayers he's missed and lays so hopelessly in bed.

Oh Allah,
he's so afraid to read,
the wisdom that's revealed may burrow in his mind.
He'll be obliged to admit,
He'll be obliged to submit,
but will he be strong enough to live the truth he finds?
Oh Allah,
he's so afraid to read.

I sent an email to my loved one, just the other day,
it's sad communication has evolved this way.
We use so many words but have so little to relay,
as angels scribble down every letter that we say.
All the viral attachments sent and passionate insults we vent,
it's easy to be arrogant behind user passwords we invent.
But on the day the scrolls are laid,
with every word and deed displayed,
when we read our accounts,
I know,
for one,
I'll be afraid.

That day,
I'll be so afraid to read,
every harsh word that I've spoken – and every time I have lied.
I'll be obliged to admit,
I'll be obliged to submit,
will I have strength owning up to each deed I've tried to hide?
Oh Allah,
I'm so afraid to read.

Flying

His body is heavy, his body is clumsy,
it won't lighten up to lift him off the sidewalk.
He's walking then running,
arms outstretched jumping,
he reaches the low limbs but he can't pluck the moon down.

There goes Ralph again.

He always pretended that he was a hero,
he was a man who could fly like a seagull.
But he is a turtle, he's slow and he's tired
and it's getting to be that his shell it is empty.

There goes Ralph again.

We read in the papers, say that he was crazy,
his home-made cape was caught in the tree boughs.
He thought he could fly out of the window,
we thought that we told him that he was no hero.

But he will be high above flying and floating,
and he will be high above laughing and gloating.
Perhaps he loved life, but just wanted to fly,
and you must give up one for the sake of the other.
It's too bad to choose but you must die to fly.

There goes Ralph again and he's flying.

All These Pictures

The kitchen table is crowded,
with piles of freshly washed clothes.
The month of June,
spills in through the windows.
You're singing a song,
of a white sheep on a blue hill.
I sit with some crayons,
drawing pictures of my world for you.
You can hang them on your fridge door,
for everyone to see.

The radio is quiet,
underneath your humming song.
The iron is steaming.
I can tell you're tired but calm.
My cola is sweating,
leaves a ring on my page.
I bounce to the window
and squint at the sun.
Proudly hang this on your fridge door,
for everyone to see.

Bird on the trough
of the eve outside the glass,
beyond his perch
across the toy cluttered grass,
above your waiting green lawn chair,
the poplars applaud
the song I hear from a hiding tree-toad.
I watch you hang up the wet linen,
on the clothes-line in the yard.

All these pictures.
You can hang them on your fridge door,
for everyone to see.

Proudly hang them on your fridge door,
as you watch me leave.

Hang my post cards on your fridge door,
to remind you of me.

History and Handshake Kisses

You shook my hand with all the power of your history,
but it felt just like a kiss to me.

To say 'I love you', God knows I've tried.
Slipped my own hand quickly back inside my pocket,
to keep your handshake kiss always safe and by my side.

You said I would be late,
so I hurried through the gate.

Somewhere Down My Street

Somewhere down my street,
young men on ten speeds,
remind me of you.
This block of world is so small.

A girl in a jean skirt,
surrounded by other laughing girls,
been admired,
somewhere down my street.

Young men stare,
reminding me how,
we took the long way around.
Somewhere down my street.

Driving down my street,
in my mirror I see snow,
exhaust clouds the past.
This block of world is so small.

We stay behind,
somewhere down my street.
This block of world is so small.

Memories of William

Tall weeds brushed against our knees.
You said we were giants crushing trees.
The fire roared, I sat and watched you play.
The end of a perfect day.
We tucked all of our words away.

The night was black. I could not see.
You took my hand and through the trees you guided me.
We sang and strummed so long, so strong, so free.
Good to laugh so late with you,
Good to laugh. What else could we do?

Tromping through fields of memories.
You said we were heroes following dreams.
The fire roared, I watched you slip to sleep.
The end of a perfect day.
Sticks and stars burn then fade away.

Stuffed Animals Behind My Bed

I picked up and dusted off the stuffed toys,
from where they fell and hid behind my bed.
I had not seen their smiles in a long time.
I had almost passed them up for dead.
I found your number in my book – so I thought I'd give you a call.
You were out with the boys.
Sometimes I cannot recall your face at all.
But sometimes I hear your voice.

And that's the way it goes, sometimes.
And that's the way it goes.

And soon my raft is setting off for a happier island,
and I'd like you to jump aboard, but you're standing on the shore.
Soon I will be born into this ocean, and I don't want you to cut
    the cord.
(Swim over anytime.)

But that's the way it goes, sometimes.
And that's the way it goes.

No – I don't want you to cut the cord.
But soon I will be born into this ocean,
and you're standing on the shore.

Soon.
So soon – I will be born.

Albert

Feels like I've known you for a life-time now,
though we met just a few years ago.
We've lost our heads more than a few times now,
but we always seem to get back in the know.

So many times that I have hung up on you.
As many times, I think, you've done that to me.
So many times, it seemed, I hated to be around you.
While, in the back of my mind, I knew no place I'd rather be.

I wish that I could hear you – now that I'm here alone,
though I think I still know all there is to know about you.
All those adventures – overturning every stone.
Is there another place left for us to go?

Love Strong
(written with Bill Kocher)

He's moping and scrubbing.	Why?
She's chatting and smiling.	Why cry?
He's studying and sipping.	Why comply?
She's a hockey fan.	Why? Why?

Why are you anxious for something?	Why?
Why are they looking out for you?	Why spy?
You're backpedaling.	Why?
Why are they all coming in now?	Why? Why pry?

We all want a simple song.	(Truth has been confused.
We all want to get along.	Simplicity refused.
We all want to just belong.	This trust has been abused.
We all want to know right from wrong.	So how am I to love,
We all want to love and be loved strong.	and be loved strong?)

He's purchasing sweetness.	Why?
Why is he paying for a pick-me-up?	Why try?
She's naturally pretty, she's socially shy,	
she's glazed her smile on.	Why? Why lie?

We all want a simple song.   (Truth has been confused.
We all want to get along.   Simplicity refused.
We all want to just belong.   This trust has been abused.
We all want to know right from wrong. So how am I to love,
We all want to love and be loved strong.   and be loved strong?)

The moment is trapped now in all of our clothes,
where we're all going we're standing in rows.
Right now we're waiting, biding our time.
The daylight is fading.   Why? Why? Why?

We all want a simple song.   (Truth has been confused.
We all want to get along.   Simplicity refused.
We all want to just belong.   This trust has been abused.
We all want to know right from wrong. So how am I to love,
We all want to love and be loved strong.   and be loved strong?)

The Sweetest Afternoon

Puppets, painters, poets, potters,
storytellers, dancers, clowns:
boiling, burning in the sun,
enchanting, sweating, singing, panting.

And it's something just as simple as you with your new freckles,
and the tapping of your sandal to a tune,
that occupies my thoughts and eyes,
for the entire afternoon.

Midnight

He sat back in his arrogant sort of way.
He said, 'There's nothing more to say',
then lectured on for another hour.

She said everything was fine.
She said she didn't like to whine,
then cried on for another hour.

They sat there screaming through the room was silent.
They sat so still, though the scene was violent.
And words can never really help you say,
what you want them to anyway.
And words can never really help you see,
what you really want to be.
He took a last sip of cold tea.

Last chance to stop all these lies.
Last chance to clean up these lives.
This could be the final hour.

This could be the final hour,
or this could be the finest hour.

And words can never really help you say,
what you want them to anyway.
And words can never really help you see,
what you really want to be.

He took a last sip of cold tea.

Sun Snow

There was nothing more to say.
There was sun-snow as I drove away.
Back home was the only place to go,
            and I did not know,
                    I would never see her after that day.

Black Glass

You need not tell me I'm crazy.
I can see you in the black glass.
I look at you, alone in this room,
just as you view me.
You in the black glass.

Yes, I'll find a way away,
out of all this,
you in the black glass.
So tomorrow I can look through you,
at morning.

You need not tell me I'm crazy,
I can see.
You in the black glass.

Move to See (Prayer of a Derelict)

Walking down the street.
Puddles at the edge of the road.
Everything seems to repeat.
How was it, I was born into this hole?
And it's cold.
Leaves are blowing and it's cold.
My hair is growing,
my life is going.
Growing old.

Where do I go?
Move to see.
Move to be.
Move to me,
if you're there.

Argus Array
(written with Bill Kocher)

What kind of people can't keep it in their heads?
What kind of dreams are left in these beds?
Bleach in the sheets is familiar and sweet,
like Saturday laundry mornings on my mum's old street.

How many mes have sat in this chair?
How many mes have slept there?

Without doubt coming out or saying anything too free,
I'd like to understand what it would be like to be me.
One song of optimism, to understand this mission.
Being so self-protecting, put in this position.

How many mes have looked out this window?
How many mes have made this room home?

This bed, this chair, this window, the bleach, this song, this room,
they change depending on my angle, gaze or mood.
My street, Saturlaundryday is all I see when I think.
Is this, or was that, home? Wonderwash my clothes in the sink.

How many mes have sat in this chair?
How many mes have slept there?
How many mes have looked out this window?
How many mes have made this room home?
How many mes have made their way home?

The Last Tea Song (Truth and the Silent Voice)

Lips no longer singing,
I watch them kiss the tea cup.
A silent voice by choice.

Quick pace with gentle gestures.
Black hair, grey strands of knowledge.
Smiling eyes, so wise.
A silent voice by choice.

I did not always favour
the choice of words,
but I enjoyed the rhymes sometimes.
Concluding truth is buried,
deep inside of men,
sweep away each day.

A silent voice by choice.

Upon My Shelf

I was sure you smiled at me when I saw you through the screen.
Your voice seems older now than the voice I recall.
The smile of a young girl I remember,
kept me warm,
back when February chilled my museless mind.

> She sings, 'These are days we'll remember',
> see them spinning into change.
> I wish I could have known you,
> before you became so far away.

When I was eighteen, he helped to calm my temper.
Helped to ease my mind, he may have even kept me sane.
Then I read he stopped it all and then he stole away.
Hid himself under a new face and he went and changed his name
   again.

> She sings, 'These are days we'll remember',
> see them spinning into change.
> I wish I could have known you,
> before you became so far away.

No more starry eyes from behind these dusty spectacles.
I'll wipe them and follow my own shadow for a change.

Who knows, someday we may all be content with this mess.
I'll thank you for your comfort and pray for you happiness.
Until then, I'll keep a spot for you upon my shelf,
and I'll keep you in my eyes just like a part of myself.

> I'll sing, 'These are days we'll remember',
> see them spinning into change.
> I'll get to know myself,
> before I get too far away.

Lives Cross

It was 6.30 in the morning,
I was driving my car in the country,
when I saw her walking by the side of the road.

She looked at me as I drove by,
a lazy gaze and faking shy.
She flipped her face up to the sky,
and gave her untied curls a toss.

It was her hair that caught me,
the shoes in each hand she carried,
her bare feet shuffling through the dew.

She smiled at me from through her hair,
my car threw dust and gravel in the air,
both of us lost in 'who knows where'.
Ain't it crazy how some lives cross?

Dark Heba

Mask your shape beneath your veils,
hide yourself away.
Mysteries that you conceal,
set my mind at play.

You stare so long, you stare so strong,
deep into my soul.
You grin so brightly, sensually wrong,
to make my heart your goal.

Oh Heba! Dark Heba!
I raise my gaze to the sky.
Oh Heba! Dark Heba!
So modestly you're so sly.

My desire and God's hell-fire,
burn eternally on.
You drift past and float away,
like many an unwritten song.

Oh Heba! Dark Heba!
I lower my gaze to the floor.
Oh Heba! Dark Heba!
My faith is a captive of war.

Tea in St. Pancras Station

Closed my eyes, felt sleep,
the scenes were all in colour.
Awoke to see you at the end of the line –
did not recognize you immediately.
The dreams we see in reality
aren't always what they seem to be.

>The air is clearing,
>as rain washes down.
>I know Allah is hearing.
>I feel the angels all around.
>And we're whisked away with the minutes,
>and we're ticking away with the day.

Tasting bitterness,
I hear it from your lips.
Lower my gaze from the fear in your eyes.
Remove your armour,
let me take off my disguise.

The air is clearing,
as rain washes down.
I know Allah is hearing.
I feel the angels all around.
And we're whisked away with the minutes,
and we're ticking away with the day.

There's no more fearing,
as day washes down.
I know Allah is hearing,
I feel the angels all around.
And we're whisked away with the minutes,
and we're skipping away with the day...
dripping away with the rain...
ticking away with the train.

Beauty and Colour

Poems and paper napkin flowers,
I could sit and listen to you for hours,
as I simply sip my tea – so sweet and brown –
you fascinate me.
4.45, I watch the sun rise over my steering wheel.
Review mirror reflects the light in my eyes.
I can't explain this night or how I feel.

Let Allah take your hand and please grant me the other,
I will show you a world I would trust with no other.
There is so much spontaneity I need to free,
and so much beauty and colour in you,
I hope will influence me.

You watch me in a crowd,
and you worry I'm a whisper among all that is loud.
Then there is you – a song –
full of wonder and life,
and it is clear to see,
I want you as my wife.

Let Allah take your hand and please grant me the other,
I will be your father if you'll be my mother.
There's so much simplicity I want you to see,
and so much beauty and colour in you,
I hope will influence me.

Gone (Yukon Sydney) (written with Bill Kocher)

Yukon Sydney,
it's about time.
Religious weekly diary,
started on New Year's Day.
Commit your calendar plans,
seasons outwit your hands.

8 am repair man,
between the rental moves.
Five hundred kilometres,
by the light of the moon.
Plants and boxes,
left for BC that day.

Tragic distance.
Family pencilled in.
Mastering Timeless Wisdom,
is so hard to begin.
'Touching in to stay' you say,
as you're leaving again.
Too far gone too far.
So far gone.

Yukon Sydney,
you must account,
for always planning forward,
yet somehow missing out.
Looking for golden veins (gold in vain?)
lost in the hills with just your pulse.
Too far gone too far,
too far gone too far.
So far gone.

Everyday

Every morning I see you stand by the door.
Every morning you need my time, everyday you want more.
I will give you my life.
Everyday, I'll give you my life.

Every morning you see me in the breakfast window light.
Every morning is the sunny end of last night.
Everyday you stir my tea for me and everyday I go away again
    alone
and every afternoon we wonder when I'll be home,
I will give you my life.
Everyday, I'll give you my life.

> Everyday I want you here beside me,
> for it feels like I may never find my way
> into your life,
> everyday.
> Games of eye-spy down the line,
> guessing colours of our lives – hard to find.
> Hear you hum once I hang up.
> Can you guess the song still in my mind?

Every picture you give me I save,
and every colour you use is so true to you.
Every minute we spend I engrave,
and every memory rethought is so new.

There is trust that we must recognize.
There is so much that we must learn to see and be,
if we could only open our minds.
Just grow with God and please be patient with me,
and I will give you my life.

Everyday,
I'll give you my life.

Scarborough

I could be a millionaire right now.
I could be smiling at the moon.
I could be anything other than what I am,
if I wouldn't have given up so soon.

> But I'm here in this grocery line,
> with Chicklets around me,
> and if I were to step out of line,
> I'd only find parking lots and traffic jams.

I could be married to a Mediterranean princess.
I could be getting a tattoo.
I could be drinking maple syrup or coconut milk,
or doing anything sweeter than arguing with you.

> But I'm here at this bank machine,
> think I forgot my PIN again,
> and if I were to step out of line
> I'd only find parking lots and traffic jams.

I could be strumming on my front porch in the rain.
I could be in England again.
Could have made my way to Katmandu.
It might have, hurt or cut somewhat, but I should have been true.

    Instead – I'm here on hold again,
    pushed the wrong button 'good-bye',
    and if I were to step out of line
    I'd only find parking lots and traffic jams.

Block (written with Bill Kocher)

Words that don't mean,
weeds up to your waist.
Losing your time,
leads to be displaced.
Do you push on,
trying to tough talk?
One more notch made,
last line that you chalk.

    Yesterday,
    and you wonder why,
    dust has settled down and you can not breathe.
    Work for space, but will you accept the sky?
    This moon is coming down if you know what I mean.

Chalk one up now,
for the pleasure it fades.
Anchors down here,
absent through the grades.
Do you push on,
words up to your waist?
Notching your loss,
last line to displace?

Yesterday,
and you wonder why,
dust has settled down and you cannot breathe.
Work for space, but will you accept the sky?
This moon is coming down if you know what I mean.

Looks hard when it's pulp to the touch.   (*Blame* always
Pick up the pen and start again.   *falls* over
Looks hard when you think too much.   *on* those
Pick up the pen and start again.   *you* know.)

Yesterday,
and you wonder why,
dust has settled down and you cannot breathe.
Work for space, but will you accept the sky?
This moon is coming down if you know what I mean.

The Poets

If he were speaking truth,
he'd confess he wasted youth,
on chasing old stray cats and sporting fashion hats,
if he could speak the truth.

If he could tell a lie,
he'd say that he knew why,
he does all we see him do.
Don't think he fools me or you,
if he could tell a lie.

But the poets say one thing and do another.
Shake the hands of the pious men then slap the face of a child's
    mother.
Words leaked from the pen,
bring wonder from ladies, envy from men,
just as smooth as sweet brown tea.

If he could read a line,
just understand one sign.
Close his mouth and hear the peace of hope and fear,
if he could read a line.
If he could keep in time.

But the poets say one thing and do another.
Shake the hands of the pious men then eat the flesh of their dead
 brother.
Words leaked from the pen,
bring wonder from ladies, envy from men,
just as smooth as sweet profanity.

Profanity like poetry.

The Prophet's Hands

(written with Zain Bhikha and Yusuf Islam)

Holding to the wheel,
each mile closer to conclusion.
His knuckles and his strands of hair are slowly turning white.
As he studies all the lines,
like highways on his hands,
while recalls how straight the road once seemed,
as he is left wondering what's right.
The paths all curve and bend,
sometimes he thinks they'll never end.
How much longer will he push on?
How much more can he pretend?

The prophet's hands,
silken smooth and soft to touch,
sometimes he needs those hands so much,
to feel them clasp his own,
let him know he's not alone.
The prophet's hands,
if they could take over the reigns,
if they could take away the strains,
guide him to the end with the patience of a friend.
Oh Allah, sometimes he needs the prophet's hands.

Stepping out to work each day,
come whatever weather.
Father of the house he holds worry in his hands.
While she stays home left all alone,
hands warn from too much ironing,
T.V. churns out but illusions –
claims to know but cannot understand.
They greet but hardly meet,
upon an endless dead-end street,
while children break the stormy silence
of the palms raised in defeat.

The prophet's hands,
silken smooth and soft to touch,
sometimes they need those hands so much,
to feel them clasp their own,
let them know they're not alone.
The prophet's hands,
can bind husband and wife,
remind them why they share a life,
clasp them both upon his heart,
gently help them make a start to hold each other,
as they'd hold the prophet's hands.

Standing in the market square,
so alive but void of life.
We work and we sweat and we struggle through each day.
As our efforts scar our hands,
this world stains us with demands.
It's hard to see life's humour in the business games we play.
As we gnaw our nails with stress,
our fists and hearts pound so carelessly.
With every effort forward,
how much more can we digress?

The prophet's hands,
silken smooth and soft to touch,
sometimes we needs those hands so much,
to feel them clasp our own,
let us know we're not alone.
The prophet's hands,
as we toil in the square,
come up behind us unaware.
Playful palms across our eyes,
teasing to help us realize,
we need the jesting, joking, calming
prophet's hands.

The prophet's hands,
silken smooth and soft to touch,
sometimes we needs those hands so much,
to feel them clasp our own
and let us know we're not alone.
The prophet's hands,
if they could take over the reigns,
if they could take away the strains,
guide us to the end with the patience of a friend.
Oh Allah, sometimes we need the prophet's hands.
Oh Allah, sometimes we need the prophet's hands.
Oh Allah, sometimes I miss the prophet's hands.

Dip in the Shallow End (written with Bill Kocher)

I'm trying to find someplace to breathe,
but I'll just skip that for now.
You're phoning, talking, emailing, knocking me down.
How long should I stay around?

And it's leaving me tired this morning.
Windows open, freeze me out of bed.
And it's leaving me crazed, emotions flail with no warning,
and I'm watching someone else move into my head.

I'm trying to find the right time to leave,
but I'll just skip lunch for now.
Lonely and closed and I think we all know why.
Should I give up before you start to try?

And it's leaving me tired this morning.
Windows open, freeze dreams in the head.
And it's leaving me crazed, emotions flare with no warning,
and I'm watching someone else move into my bed.

And it's leaving me tired and I'm warning.
Windows open, freeze my hands on the ledge.
And it's leaving me sad that you just can't see the morning.
And I'm watching each night fall now, upon edge.

I'm trying to find the right time to leave,
but I'll stare out the window for now.
You're sleeping there, still so unaware.
I'm getting dressed without a sound.

And it's leaving me tired this morning.
Windows open, freeze me out of bed.
And it's leaving me dazed, and I reflect on the warning,
as I'm watching someone else move into my bed.
Move into my head.
Move into my bed.

For You in Fez

I don't think I fell,
I think I jumped this time.
Don't quite know if I'm flailing or I'm flying,
wondering if I'll land alive.
I can see you smile,
but it doesn't ease my mind.
I can see you run like a puppy,
bounding way ahead,
wondering if I'll lag behind.

Now you're here,
and there's nothing that's unclear,
can't you hear my fear,
subliminally insecure?
I've told you all I can,
now you and God know I'm a simple man.

Now I'm wondering what the hell
will inspire my next rhyme.
Wondering if my words or fingertips will weave
or leave maze-like prints of crime.
If how you feel is real,
and if what we do is true,
how should I balance these emotions
between tradition or you?

And you're here,
and there's nothing that's unclear.
Can't you hear my fear,
subliminally insecure?
I've told you how I feel,
God knows what simple hearts conceal.

No Time for Rhyme

I cannot want to justify,
the waste of dripping ink and time,
making a try that is a lie,
to hunt for words of love that rhyme.

      Now there's no time for rhyme.
      No time for rhyme.
      Each word is one step further from each thought
      that I could say,
      and there's no time for rhyme today.

To grasp our time before it goes,
struggling with metre will not do,
I will compose for you a prose,
to share my words of love for you.

      Now there's no time for rhyme.
      No time for rhyme.
      Each word is one step further from each thought
      that I could say,
      and there's no time for rhyme today.

If I'm a poet as professed,
true to my soul, my life and art,
the words are best that can't be guessed,
in my attempt to pen my heart.

No minute wasting rhymes from me,
for time and words, please understand,
must always be passionately,
seized in the way I seize your hand.

      Now there's no time for rhyme.
      No time for rhyme.
      Each word is one step further from each thought
      that I could say,
      and there's no time for rhyme today.

Troubadour

Women tell you that you are such a peculiar one.
Men tell you they'd willfully risk, being shot by your rejection.
I tell you that I've never cried so hard or had such fun.
I'm convinced that with your truth,
you could blind the sun.

> Let me be your dramatic fool.
> I'll dance – watch me stumble sing and crumble on
>   your floor,
> La la la la, consider me your court jester Troubadour.

Women tell you, 'Untangle your hair and paint your eyes.'
Fading fashion flavours and body waxing, bring smooth lies.
Baggy trousers, unkempt tresses are more your style.
I'm a crooked man with a crooked grin,
who wants to taste your crooked smile.

> Let me be your dramatic fool.
> I'll dance – watch me stumble sing and crumble on
>   your floor,
> La la la la, I am your garden bard Troubadour.

Oh, Oh, Oh – I'm in the snow for you.
Hey, hey, hey – I'm dripping with rain.
Alas, alas – I'm sleeping in long grass.
Waiting to know,
by your window.

> Let me be your dramatic fool.
> I'll dance – watch me stumble sing and crumble on
>   your floor,
> La la la la, I am your merry minstrel Troubadour.

Hold the Stage

I'm a lot like my guitar case,
'Fragile Caution' across my face.
But the stickers go ignored.
Tossed up causally on board.
And when the trip is done –
and once we've come down from the sun,
all we are that's been in hold,
lands one more mile towards Old.
And as the baggage tumbles down,
conveyer belt streams toss it 'round,
capsized canoe, a cliff top drop.
Over the hill – mid-fall,
too fast to stop.

       Hold the stage.
       Nail the note.
       Building dreams with wood and wire.
       Who's a poet? Who's a liar?
       Act my age.
       Sink or float.
       Someplace between Eden and Fire,
       the scale tips higher and higher.
       Hold the stage.

A little iPod wearing shoes.
My shirt is funk. Jeans of the blues.
Jazz and country harmonize.
Open my mouth and shut my eyes.
I'd like to think there's more to be,
than just a human MP3.
More to see and more to do,
than offer up a song or two.
There's a hit I never wrote,
a song stuck sharp deep in my throat.
I could maybe breathe again if I could free it.
Stop thinking what may be,
maybe just be it.

Hold the stage.
Nail the note.
Building dreams with wood and wire.
Who's a poet? Who's a liar?
Act my age.
Sink or float.
Someplace between Eden and Fire,
the scale tips higher and higher.
Hold the stage.

Inside, the music's jarred.
The case so strong, to last so long,
gets scraped and scratched and gashed so fast,
before you know the song's gone past.

Hold the stage.
Hold on strong.
Living a dream waiting to wake.
How much to give? How much to take?
Shake my cage.
The bars of song.
Someplace between Eden and Fire,
the scale tips higher and higher.
Hold the stage.

I'm a lot like my guitar case.
Another scuff...never enough.
Hold the plane.

Wisdom and Tea

I'm looking back throughout the years,
to breathe is hard and my eyes are choked with tears.
Your face and hair are full of light, now it will soon be time to go.
I sense you feeling calm now. Did the angel let you know?

For all the wisdom and tea you gave to me,
let me offer something now, so warm and comforting and sweet.
Can you hear me whisper to you as you sleep?
'*La ilaha illallah.*' Did you always understand?
Can you feel me take your hand?

Flowers, house plants and I – you helped us grow,
now as I hold your cup – how were you and I to know,
I'd care for you and look for hints of paradise as I bend to wash
    your feet?
Our minutes fade like photographs or crowds from an evening
    street.

For all the wisdom and tea you gave to me,
let me offer something now, so warm and comforting and sweet.
Can you hear me whisper to you as you sleep?
'*La ilaha illallah.*' Did you always understand?
Can you feel me take your hand?

I dreamt we sat in the kitchen like we used to, having tea,
the apparition vanished, as in life's reality.
'We will meet again,' is what I'm sure I heard you say,
'on the day when veils and secrets of the heart will be torn away.'

For all the wisdom and tea you gave to me,
let me offer something now, so warm and meaningful and sweet.
Can you hear me whisper to you as you sleep?
'*La ilaha illallah.*' Did you always understand?
As I let go of your hand? For all the wisdom and tea you gave to me,
let me turn to something now, so warm and comforting and
    sweet.
Allah give us peace in our final sleep.
La ilaha illallah. Give us patience to understand.
Ya Ghafur, Ya Rahman!

What is finally in the heart?
What is the final choice?
Allah knows, and all that we can claim,
are just memories of a voice.

Shady Grove (Based on traditional lyrics)

Shady Grove, my little love, Shady Grove my love.
Shady Grove, my little love, I'm bound for Shady Grove.

> First time I saw my Shady Grove, standing by the door.
> Shoes and stockings in her hand and little bare feet on
> the floor.

> Next I saw my Shady Grove, running down the path.
> I love to see her smiling eyes and I love to hear her laugh.

Shady Grove, my little love, Shady Grove my love.
Shady Grove, my little love, I'm bound for Shady Grove.

> Last I saw my Shady Grove, by the river's foam.
> Water took my world away and left me all alone.
> The waves washed my world away and left me all alone.

Shady Grove, my little love, Shady Grove I say.
Shady Grove, my little love, why'd you go away?

> Peaches in the summertime, apples in the fall,
> if I can't have the girl I love I won't have none at all.

> You'll find me in the Shady Grove, living on my own.
> I feel my love in the shadows there and I'm never all alone.
> I hear her laugh in the Shady Grove and I'm never all alone.

Shady Grove, my little love, Shady Grove my love.
Shady Grove, my little love, I'm bound for Shady Grove.

Rachel

First time I saw Rachel, I looked deep into her eyes.
My reflection there was a gaping stare,
as I watched her laugh in that photograph,
and time between us lost somewhere.

First time I saw Rachel, I began to realize,
she possessed such grace in her youthful face,
sweet integrity that woke a void in me.
Now her passion breathes within that space.

> It has nothing to do with age,
> it's not our languages, religion, gender, colour of our skin.
> It's a soul within a well that echoes deep beneath the
>   ego's shell.
> True life can't ever start 'til we offer up our heart.
> As the wolves lick their teeth at the sheep in rows,
> I want to live the life that Rachel chose.

All the girls and boys, seen preening through school halls,
fighting to fit in, games we just can't win.
Higher education dumbing down a nation,
'round the square, unsure of where we fit in.

> It has nothing to do with age,
> it's not our languages, religion, gender, colour of our skin.
> It's a soul within a well that echoes deep beneath the
>   ego's shell.
> True life can't ever start 'til we offer up our heart.
> When the wolves rip the fleece from the sheep –
>   God knows,
> I want to live the life that Rachel chose.

Rachel, what so pushed you, to put so much on hold?
From a school-hall door to a need for more?
From where we all stayed, to where you last laid,
silently strong in the choices you made.

It has nothing to do with age,
it's not our languages, religion, gender, colour of our skin.
It's a soul within a well that echoes deep beneath the
    ego's shell.
True life can't ever start 'til we offer up our heart.
When hate tears the hope where the olive tree grows.
I will live the life that Rachel chose.

Let it Go

We lean like leaves toward the light.
I can almost hear them bend.
Wall clock like a metronome.
Lavender like an old friend.
And we can sew a song.
And we will let it grow.

Rolled oats simmer on the stove.
Cats are smiling all around.
Break my heart – tear it apart,
with laughter rolling on the ground.
Puts me on the road.
And we can let it go.

Here in the hive,
dance, hum and drone.

I can still see Richie now,
with his tattoos years ago.
Scratch the pirate on my arm.
Spin the wheel and let it go.
And we can let it go.

Here in the hive,
dance, hum and drone.

The past we've got we must forget.
Future hasn't happened yet.
Carry this moment in a song.
Insha Allah, it won't be long.

Allah, Allah, Allah Alhamdulillah!
Ya Subhanahu wa ta'ala.
Ya Allah.
Insha Allah.

Eight Years Old

That open pain that you looked through,
let in the storms of life that blew,
all your notes upon the ground –
took out the lights and killed the sound.
But your time has come around.

Now there's a young woman and a young man,
who fell hard while you were seeking truth.
Kisses good-bye, you kissed the sky and you kissed away their
    youth.
Some sick or sacred plan, for a young woman and young man.

Time seems cold, each day we grey away.
Believe the lines that we've been told,
'Lose our way lose yesterday', they say,
but who are they?
Who are they anyway?
They didn't hear us play
at eight years old.

A treasure map you didn't lose.
The lines to follow, if we choose.
Stand now to take the bow, we may be so surprised to learn,
there's one bridge you didn't burn.

Time seems cold, each day we grey and fray.
Believe the lies that we've been told,
'Lose our way lose yesterday', they say,
but who are they?
Who are they anyway?
They didn't hear us play
at eight years old.

We're eight years old.

PART II

TO INSPIRE

Bismillah

Bismillahir Rahmanir Rahim, alhamdulillahir Rabbil 'alamin.

In the morning when we wake, *bismillah.*
with every step we take, *bismillah.*
with every word we say, *bismillah.*
and everything that comes our way, *bismillah.*

Bismillahir Rahmanir Rahim, alhamdulillahir Rabbil 'alamin.

With everything we do, *bismillah.*
with everything that's new, *bismillah.*
with every place we go, *bismillah.*
and every one we know, *bismillah.*

Bismillahir Rahmanir Rahim, alhamdulillahir Rabbil 'alamin.

With every song we sing, *bismillah.*
from every mountain, peace will ring.

Bismillahir Rahmanir Rahim, alhamdulillahir Rabbil 'alamin.

Salam, Shalom – A Piece of Peace
(Adapted from the traditional Hebrew hymn
'Shalom My Friend')

> *Shalom* my friend, *shalom* my friend,
> *shalom, shalom.*
> May peace be with you,
> God's peace be with you,
> *Shalom. Shalom.*

* * * * *

As salamu 'alaikum!
　　　Wa 'alaikum as salam!
I greet you with a greeting of peace,
and a shake of your hand.
As salamu 'alaikum!
　　　Wa 'alaikum as salam!
I greet you with peace,
a piece of peace,
to spread throughout the land.

As we look towards the time we have left,
as we try to do what's right,
I'll greet you with peace this morning my friend,
peace through day 'til night.

As we turn to our friends and look to our left,
as we look to our dreams turning right,
I will greet you with peace when I see you my friend,
and the light of a smile will ignite.

As salamu 'alaikum!
　　　Wa 'alaikum as salam!
I greet you with a greeting of peace,
and a shake of your hand.
As salamu 'alaikum!
　　　Wa 'alaikum as salam!
I greet you with peace,
a piece of peace,
to spread throughout the land.

Sing, Children of the World

Walking through the crowded streets of a market in Morocco.
Sitting on a smiling camel in the desert of Arabia.
Chasing 'round the bamboo trees of Bandung, Indonesia.
Gathering brightly coloured leaves in a forest of Canada.

Napping beneath the date palm shade under blue skies of
    Tunisia.
Freeing kites into the night from a roof-top in Pakistan.
Planting rows of beans and maize on a small farm in Uganda.
Laying back to count the stars from somewhere in Afghanistan.

> Sing, Children of the World, come together and hear
>   the call!
> Sing, Children of the World, our youth will unite us all!
> Sing, Children of the World, the truth will unite us all!
> *Subhanallah walhamdulillah wallahu akbar*!

Splashing through the pouring rain in a village of Guyana.
Nibbling cakes from picnic plates on a mountaintop in
    Switzerland.
Tending to a flock of sheep down under in Australia.
Greeting morning with a prayer on the golden Egyptian sand.

> Sing, Children of the World, come together and hear
>   the call!
> Sing, Children of the World, our youth will unite us all!
> Sing, Children of the World, the truth will unite us all!
> *Subhanallah walhamdulillah wallahu akbar*!

Crying himself to sleep, with no hope left for dreaming.
Begging in the burning sun, holding out her hand.
Palms held tightly on his ears to muffle all the screaming.
Sitting where her house once stood, trying hard to understand.

See the children of the World...all the children of the World.
Sing for the children of the World.
Pray for the children of the World.

> Sing, Children of the World, come together and hear
>   the call!
> Sing, Children of the World, our youth will unite us all!
> Sing, Children of the World, the truth will unite us all!
> *Subhanallah walhamdulillah wallahu akbar!*

Hi Neighbour! Salam Neighbour!
(with thanks to Abdul Malik Mujahid)

> *Salam* Neighbour! Hi!
> Let's get together you and I.
> A new day has just begun,
> you call the rain, I'll call the sun,
> and we can sing and we can splash,
> and we can shine down on the grass.
> Believe in make-believe, long as we can!
> Hi neighbour! *Salam*!

I think dandelions roar with beauty.
I think being free is my duty.
We've got to take a chance,
fly by the seat of our proverbial pants.
There's so much we can do,
out in this world, me and you.
There's so much we can improve,
if you dig my drift,
if you catch my groove.

Salam Neighbour! Hi!
Let's get together you and I.
A new day has just begun,
you call the rain, I'll call the sun,
and we can sing and we can splash,
and we can shine down on the grass.
Believe in make-believe, long as we can!
Hi neighbour! *Salam*!

There are a lot of grown ups who,
should be sent up to their rooms,
and told they must stay there,
until they learn they can play fair.
There are a lot of kids like me,
and a lot of kids like you,
who know kindness and trust,
make friends like one plus one make two.

Hi Neighbour! *Salam*!
Let's pack a picnic lunch and scram!
We can go out near some trees,
you bring the bread, I'll bring the cheese.
You beat the drum, I'll sing the song,
and all the forest will sing along.
We'll watch parades of ants and birds
and clouds pass by,
Salam Neighbour! Hi!

Salam Neighbour! Hi!
Let's get together you and I.
A new day has just begun,
you call the rain, I'll call the sun,
and we can sing and we can splash,
and we can shine down on the grass.
Believe in make-believe, long as we can!
Hi neighbour! *Salam*!

Window Song

My window is an everlasting motion picture screen.
It's kind of an epic that lasts for hours and hours and hours.
It's got lots of stars and someone's sun,
and lots of prop trees and cars and flowers, flowers, flowers.

Every morning the motion picture begins,
and sometimes it's a little brighter than other days.
And sometimes it's a dark comedy that really isn't funny.
I wonder if the being who made this motion picture,
just did it for fun, or was it commissioned a lot of money?

And when the credits roll by,
it'll be on the day I die,
and it will say who it's directed by,
and if it's there for me to re-see...or re-read...or re-be.

My window is an everlasting motion picture screen.
It's kind of an epic that lasts for hours and hours and hours
    and hours and hours.
I have no need to pay admission,
and if I did that would be pretty unfair,
considering I'm in the motion picture too,
and so are you.

Rhythm of Surrender

Can you hear the rhythm of all creation?
The rhythm of the clapping of the thunder and the rain?
Can you see the rhythm of all creation?
The lightening and the leaves and the seasons as they change?

Watch the children in the field, spinning 'round and 'round.
Watch their lanky, laughing, dizzy, silly falls upon the ground.
They grip on to long grass afraid of spinning with the sun.
Reality deceives them 'neath a smiling mask of fun.

Can you hear the rhythm of all creation?
The rhythm of the children aging brown hair into grey?
Can you see the rhythm of all creation?
Alternation of the moon and stars passing into day?

Watch the grown ups all twirling with the clock throughout the
    day.
Watch them spinning through the hours while the time hands
    tick away.
They talk and grip the world, as they would catch a falling knife.
Reality deceives them 'neath amusing games of life.

Can you hear the rhythm of all creation?
The storm against the sand and the pulsating waves?
Can you see the rhythm of all creation?
The rhythm of the children running wind upon the graves?

The rhythm of our world beats in surrender and in time,
our blood and our breathing testify.
The rhythm of surrender is a part of who we are,
with each heartbeat and involuntary blink of our eye,
a part of us we can't deny.

Can you hear the rhythm of Allah's creation?
The rhythm of the clapping of the thunder and the rain?
Can you see the rhythm of Allah's creation?
The lightening and the leaves and the seasons as they change?

Sustainable Earth

The Light,
The Thunder,
The Dunes of Sand,
The Sun,
The Moon,
Man and
the land.
If we work a little, we might see,
if we think and reflect on each rock and tree,
there's no measure to all it's worth,
sustainable earth.

The Ant,
The Spider,
The Gnat,
The Bee,
The Cow,
The Cattle,
The Unity.
If we care a little, you and me,
if we play our part in ecology,
there's no measure to all it's worth,
sustainable earth.

We are a new generation,
the task has just begun.
We can be the strongest nation,
caretakers of the world – everyone.
Sustainable earth.

Colours of Islam

Allah made us all a different shade and colour.
Nations and tribes recognize one another!
'Cause every single person is your sister and brother.
So many different colours of *islam*.

>Fill the world with colour, paint it everywhere you go.
>Paint everything you see, and tell everyone you know.
>Qur'an will be your paint, and your brush will be *iman*,
>so fill the world with colour, every colour of *islam*.

Truth as clear and blue as the sky we walk under.
Love as bright and loud as the lightening and thunder.
Peace as pure and white as the moon, so full of wonder.
So many different colours of *islam*!

>Fill the world with colour, paint it everywhere you go.
>Paint everything you see, and tell everyone you know.
>Qur'an will be your paint, and your brush will be *iman*,
>so fill the world with colour, every colour of *islam*.

Smiles, warm and shining, like the sun upon our faces.
Hope as rich and green as the trees of an oasis.
The colours of *islam* bloom in so many places.
So many different colours of *islam*.

>Fill the world with colour, paint it everywhere you go.
>Paint everything you see, and tell everyone you know.
>Qur'an will be your paint, and your brush will be *iman*,
>so fill the world with colour, every colour of *islam*.

Wide World

Forge a forest,
cross the sand,
take a trip,
you can hold my hand through,
this wide world.

See the cities,
share the land,
board my ship the path is planned through,
this wide world.

Everybody's here living on this sphere,
spinning on this world so wild and wide.
We can learn and think and go,
discover all there is to know,
about what's all around us and what's beautiful inside,
of our wide world.

It's your wide world.
It's my wide world.
This wonderful wide world.

Rain (Life Returns)

The earth is hard.
Soil is cracked, bleached and blistered.
Trees bend, withered and weary.
Ground gasps, dusty and dry.
God hears and the rains come,
wetting and washing the world.
Flushing and flooding the clay,
spilling and splashing,
life returns.

We are the cracked earth,
the thirsty, dirty spirit of man.
If we gasp, we will be heard.
Forgiveness falls like rain on our hands.
God hears and the rains come,
wetting and washing the world.
Flushing and flooding the clay,
spilling and splashing,
life returns.

Theeverythingsong

I'm gonna take my bicycle and ride out to a field,
and play under the sky with the mosquitoes and the birds.
We can play together, you can come with me.
Have you ever made *azan*, standing high up in a tree?

Every single blade of grass,
and every day and month that pass,
and every coloured leaf,
that decorates the fall.
Every flake of snow is different,
every place you go is different,
everyone you know is different,
that's the beauty of it all.

There are a million picture puzzle pieces in the passing clouds,
we can contemplate and dream upon the beauty of their signs.
I like to lay down with my head upon the grass,
laughing with the moon and winking back at stars that pass.

Every single star you see,
and every rock within the sea,
and every drop of rain,
that you've ever felt fall.
Every flake of snow is different,
every place you go is different,
everyone you know is different,
that's the beauty of it all.

Every print on every finger of each human on the earth,
is different from each other finger print since the start of time.
Nadia speaks with her hands, not a sound comes from her lips.
Abdullah doesn't use his eyes, reads with his finger tips.

Every face and you and me,
and every stripe on every bee,
every creature that you see,
swim, fly, run, or crawl,
every flake of snow is different,
every place you go is different,
everyone you know is different,
that's the beauty of it all.

Little Bird

Little Bird, where has your mother gone?
Why are you here all alone?
Little bird where is your nest?
Why are you so far from all the rest?
Allah knows the language you speak,
and Allah can lift you high.
Allah can bring you home again,
for Allah is stronger than I,
Allah is stronger than I.

Little Bird, I wish I could,
understand the words you speak.
I wish that you could spend the day with me,
we could sit and chat as you perch upon my knee.
Allah knows the language you speak,
and Allah can lift you high.
Allah can bring you home again,
for Allah is stronger than I,
Allah is stronger than I.

Little Bird, I'd love to take you home.
Little Bird, your eyes enchant me so.
Smiling moons in the dark night sky,
I wish that I could lift you up to fly.
Allah knows the language you speak,
and Allah can lift you high.
Allah can bring you home again,
for Allah is stronger than I,
Allah is stronger than I.

I'll tell you a secret my Little Bird,
sometimes I feel alone just like you.
But we should always know, Allah is nearby,
to hear each word we pray and kiss each tear we cry.
Allah knows the language we speak,
and Allah will lift us high.
Allah will bring us home again,
for Allah is stronger than you and I.

Allah is stronger than I.

The Blue Sky is Blue (Like Blue Bubble Gum)
(with thanks to Imran Al-Bakhkam)

> The blue sky is blue like blue bubble gum,
> but it prays to Allah, it prays to Allah,
> and like the flavour of the blue sky and the bubble gum
>   won't last,
> we've got to thank Allah before our chances go past.

I don't wanna be a grown-up like the grown-ups I have seen,
'cause the grown-ups I have seen don't seem to have much fun.
They don't get down on the floor enough to pray or play with toys,
when I'm a grown-up, I won't want to be one.

Now, if I lived back at the time of the prophet,
I know he would be different, I just know he'd find the time and
I would make him something, special like a paper plane or
    something,
I could race that plane with him or get a camel back ride.

> The blue sky is blue like blue bubble gum,
> but it prays to Allah, it prays to Allah,
> and like the flavour of the blue sky and the bubble gum
>   won't last,
> we've got to thank Allah before our chances go past.

I'd like to write a promise, I want you to make it too,
that if I misbehave a little, like I sometimes do,
you won't get really mad and you'll be patient like the prophet.
I really love my promise. How about you?

> The blue sky is blue like blue bubble gum,
> but it prays to Allah, it prays to Allah,
> and like the flavour of the blue sky and the bubble gum
>   won't last,
> we've got to thank Allah before our chances go past.

To be a Mommy or a Daddy must be really, really hard,
so let's take a break together, 'cause I know how much you try.
Let's have a dish of applesauce, then tumble in the yard,
and we can pray and we can play along with the blue sky.

> The blue sky is blue like blue bubble gum,
> but it prays to Allah, it prays to Allah,
> and like the flavour of the blue sky and the bubble gum
>   won't last,
> we've got to thank Allah before our chances go past.

A Million Stories

A million stories,
I know you've got one too,
inside your memory, inside your heart.

Don't let that story fade,
grab a pen, paper and glue,
share your mind, let it free, your world's a work of art.
And your story's about to start.

You can change the whole world,
with just one little word,
so write one down, get it ready to send.

What places have you been?
What truth have you heard?
My poem is done, but your adventures never end.
So go and pick up a pen my friend.

Full of Humility

> Put all our pride away,
> always find a gentle word to say.
> You know we shouldn't fool ourselves,
> Allah has given so much to you and me.
> Put all our pride away,
> always thank Allah when we pray.
> You know we shouldn't be full of ourselves,
> when we should be full of humility.

We're all living here together on this planet floatin' 'round the sun.
We're all equal to one another, no one's better than anyone.
The only trait we have, to weigh us all apart,
is faith only Allah can see, deep inside our heart.

> Put all our pride away,
> always find a gentle word to say.
> You know we shouldn't fool ourselves,
> Allah has given so much to you and me.
> Put all our pride away,
> always thank Allah when we pray.
> You know we shouldn't be full of ourselves,
> when we should be full of humility.

Trying hard to simply be humble and never act too proud,
it's easy to trip and stumble with your nose up above the clouds.
It's always best to be modest and keep our feet on the ground,
'cause pride can eat us up inside if we're arrogant and loud.

> Put all our pride away,
> always find a gentle word to say.
> You know we shouldn't fool ourselves,
> Allah has given so much to you and me.
> Put all our pride away,
> always thank Allah when we pray.
> You know we shouldn't be full of ourselves,
> when we should be full of humility.

Positively Thinking

Some people in this world,
wear faces tired and long.
They hate to wake up, stretch and smile,
they hear the birds but not their song.
Other people walk through streets,
with a bounce in their stride.
Seeing more than the shell of the egg,
they see the life inside.

> Positively thinking with a positive attitude.
> Looking for that silver lining,
> with no fuss, complaints or whining.
> Trust Allah and after the rain,
> the grey sky will turn blue.

Some people smell the rose,
while others fear the thorn,
for all the pain a mother feels,
a new child is born.
Look at life's stress as a test,
a challenge to break through.
How you see what happens to you,
is in your point of view.

> Positively thinking with a positive attitude.
> Looking for that silver lining,
> with no fuss, complaints or whining.
> Trust Allah and after the rain,
> the grey sky will turn blue.

We all love the sunshine, but without a raining shower,
sleepy seeds will never grow and the garden never flower.

Positively thinking with a positive attitude.
Looking for that silver lining,
with no fuss, complaints or whining.
Trust Allah and after the rain,
the grey sky will turn blue.

Learn With You

Everyday we wake up and there's something new.
Each sunrise brings a day of things to learn to do.
Sometimes it's hard to learn on our own.
It's no fun trying new things, when we're all alone.
So, I'll learn with you and you learn with me.

If I can catch on to it, so can you.
Why be afraid of trying something new?
We need someone we trust standing near.
Someone we know to give a rousing cheer.
So, I'll learn with you and you learn with me.

The Veil (with thanks to Zahra Duran)

They say, 'Oh poor girl you are so beautiful you know,
it's a shame that you cover up your beauty so.'
She just smiles and graciously responds reassuringly,
'This beauty that I have is just a simple part of me.
This body that I have, no stranger has a right to see.
These long clothes, this shawl I wear, ensure my modesty.
Faith is far less fickle than fashion, wouldn't you agree?'
This *hijab*, this mark of piety,
is an act of faith, a symbol, for all the world to see.
A simple cloth, to preserve her dignity.
So lift the veil from your heart to see the heart of purity.

They tell her, 'Girl don't you know this is the west and you are
    free?
You don't need to be oppressed, ashamed of your femininity.'
She just shakes her head and she speaks so assuredly,
'See the billboards and the magazines that line the check-out
    aisles,
with their phony painted faces and their air-brushed smiles?
Well their sheer clothes and low cut gowns, they are really not
    for me.
You call it freedom, and I call it anarchy.'
This *hijab*, this mark of piety,
is an act of faith, a symbol, for all the world to see.
A simple cloth, to preserve her dignity.
So lift the veil from your heart and see the heart of purity.

They say, 'Sister of belief you are so strong,
your scarf is a flag of this faith where you belong.'
She just drops here gaze then she smiles with humility,
'I did not wear this shall at all less than one year ago.
I've been judged, misjudged and misunderstood
by those who do not know that,
faith cannot be measured by the garments that we sew.
Beauty and faith: objects reduced to a fashion show.
This *hijab*, this mark of piety,
is an act of faith, a symbol, between my God and me.
Just a simple cloth, to preserve integrity.
So lift the veil from your heart to see the very heart of me.
Lift the veil from your heart and see the heart of purity.'

When will we lift the veil from our hearts to seek the heart of
purity?

Little Love in My Heart

I've got a little love in my heart,
    and it's here to stay.

I've got a little love in my heart,
    I wanna give it away.

I've got a little love in my heart,
    and it brightens up my way,

so I'm gonna share the little love in my heart,
    with you today.

The Letter

You don't know me, but I'm your brother of this land. You'll never know my name, never know exactly where I am. But I'm a part of you – you're a part of me too – one life saved is like all mankind. Sometimes I wonder about the people in the world. So much wealth, so many fists so tightly curled. Enough for you should be enough for two. One life lost is like all mankind.

You don't see the look of hate in soldier's eyes. You don't hear my sister cry at night. You don't smell the garbage in the street and you don't know how very little food we eat.

Not a thing belongs to you or me, it's all a trust from divine rich bounty. The tree of greed grows from a seed that's planted when we don't give.

Do you know how it feels to walk for days? Do you know how it feels to sleep in snow? Do you know what it really means to pray? Can you tell me why they took my dad away?

I don't mean to seem bold or to seem rude. I'm not begging for your shelter or your food, I'm just asking you to care and to be aware. At the very least pray for me.

Peace be with you,

Your brother of this land.

Give a Little

Give a little of yourself.
Cure your greed, purify your wealth.
Look around at where you live,
look at all the good you have to give.
Give a little of yourself.

There is a hand somewhere to hold, a mouth to feed.
There's so much that we can do for so many who are in need.
Give our time, give our wealth,
give our love, give ourselves
knowing we can change the world with every deed.

Give a little of yourself.
Cure your greed, purify your wealth.
Look around at where you live,
look at all the good you have to give.
Give a little of yourself.

Take a look at all the people everywhere,
who give with open hands and hearts that do what's fair.
Can you see the blessings fall,
on believers one and all,
who take the time to give and know it's right to care?

Give a little of yourself.
Cure your greed, purify your wealth.
Look around at where you live,
look at all the good you have to give.
Give a little of yourself.

Part III

To Remind

The People of the Boxes

Prologue

*Among the sacred texts and divine revelations we have received
to help us understand where we came from
and where we are going as a human race,
the words of God – God's glorious Recitation – are most rich
in helping us find our direction.*

*They narrate truth for all time, prophecies for our future
and stories of our past,
the history of our ancestors and the wisdom of the prophets.*

*We know of the history of Adam and Eve,
parents of humanity.*

*We know of Abraham, the father of the believers who brought
all women and men towards the worship of The One God.*

*We know of the people of Lot, the people of Noah,
the people of Thamud and the people of 'Ad.*

*We have memorized the laws of Moses
and the history of the children of Israel,
the beautiful story of Joseph and his brothers,
the inspirational Good News of Jesus – his miracles and his companions,
and we know of God's last prophet and messenger Muhammad –
how he too came to the world
as a light and a mercy for all.*

May God's peace be upon these, and all of God's chosen prophets.

*But where have they brought us?
Where are their messages now?
Is their wisdom trapped in our bookshelves,
locked in our buildings of worship,
sealed within our institutions of religion,
or hidden within our boxes of faith?*

Where are we now? Who are we now?
Are we people of belief, or have we become
The People of the Boxes?

* * * * *

There were once some people who all saw their lives like empty
    boxes.
They looked around the world, collecting up the things they
    liked.
They filled their lives and boxes with the goodies that they
    gathered,
and they all felt in control, content, and they all felt alright.

They climbed inside their boxes and settled with their trinkets.
They neither looked, nor learned much more and closed their lids
    up tight.
Once they'd fastened up their boxes, they smiled there inside,
    and they all
thought in their darkness that the world was clear and bright.

> But the world is not a box.
> There's no lid, no doors, no cardboard flaps or
>   locks,
> and everything in nature from the clouds to the
>   rocks,
> is a piece of the puzzle of the purpose of
>   mankind.
> It's a piece of the peace that we'll find.

Along came a wandering wise man whispering such words of
    truth,
who stumbled on these boxes, so separate side by side.
He knocked upon the first one saying, 'Please come out and feel
    the day.'
An answer came from deep within, 'You're not of us please go
    away.'

He approached the second box and tapped thrice on the lid saying,
'Peace to you inside, shall I show you a new way?'
Someone peeked out from a crack and said, 'You may just have a
    point,
but it's so comfy in my box, in my box here I will stay.'

> But the world is not a box.
> There's no lid, no doors, no cardboard flaps or locks,
> and everything in nature from the clouds to the rocks,
> is a piece of the puzzle of the purpose of mankind.
> It's a piece of the peace that we'll find.

He stood before the final box, a hiding face peeked out to him,
and much to his surprise, he said 'I recognize those eyes!
I see you and you see me so why not come out and be free?
Faith and flowers wilt and die if they are hidden from the sky!'

> 'Cause the world is not a box.
> There's no lid, no doors, no cardboard flaps or locks,
> and everything in nature from the clouds to the rocks,
> is a piece of the puzzle of the purpose of mankind.
> It's a piece of the peace that we'll find.

Now centuries lie between the prophets and you and I.
Civilizations are born and die each and every day.
We see good and bad and happy-sad and mad mistakes we wish
    we hadn't made
in our attempt to try and live up to their way.

But if we hide ourselves away, afraid to grow and learn,
we might wake up in the flames of the ignorance that burns,
and we'll never be much more than only casualties of war
in a struggle we can't win if we have no faith to begin.

We've got to tip the lid and let some sunlight in,

'cause the world is not a box.
There's no lid, no doors, no cardboard flaps or locks,
and everything in nature from the clouds to the rocks,
is a piece of the puzzle of the purpose of mankind.
It's a piece of the peace that we'll find.

The Story of Ibrahim

Father, oh Father, why do you do it –
why do you whittle all day?
Why do you carve those statues of wood,
and fashion those idols out of clay?

Father, oh Father, why do you do it –
why do you bow down and pray?
To all those empty gods you have made,
when there's such a far better way?

There is only one God,
La ilaha illallah.
Lord of both the earth and sky,
Who knows all the answers
to where, what and why.
There is only one god,
La ilaha illallah.

I've looked to the sky, seen the moon and stars,
come then quickly fade away.
I've seen the sun so strong and bright,
die at the end of the day.

I've seen the perfection of all creation,
in every creature and leaf,
and I don't understand any woman or man,
who denies the one true belief.

There is only one God,
La ilaha illallah,
who will not fade and will not die,
who knows all the answers
to where, what and why.
There is only one God,
La ilaha illallah.

People, oh people, why won't you heed
my call to the straight way?
Your hearts are as hard as the idols you carve.
You listen but won't hear a word that I say.

People, oh people, why put your faith
in gods of gold and wood?
They crumble away, they have no life.
They cause no harm and they do no good.

There is only one God,
La ilaha illallah.
I don't understand why you choose to deny
that Allah knows the answers
to where, what and why.
There is only one God,
La ilaha illallah.

People, oh people, you've tried to break me,
you've called me a fool and a liar.
But I will not burn in your flames,
for faith in Allah will cool any fire.

So hate me or hurt me, do what you will,
even banish me from this land,
I will pray to Allah that the truth comes to you
and I pray that some day you will all understand,

there is only one God,
La ilaha illallah.
Lord of both the earth and sky
who will not fade and who will not die.
There is only one God,
La ilaha illallah.
No, I don't understand why you choose to deny
that Allah knows the answers
to where, what and why.
There is only one God,
La ilaha illallah.

The Beautiful Story of Yusuf

We sipped our tea as he sat next to me,
cross-legged on the floor,
and he spoke of his youth thrown to the wolves,
a student of the hardship of war.
A war which shaped him and moulded him to
a grateful and God-fearing man;
the struggle of a nation burned in his eyes,
as he relived his war-torn homeland.
Accused and abused he was stolen away,
no justice exists with no law.
Like the prophet Yusuf he was thrown into prison,
but they couldn't cage his faith in Allah.

The beautiful story of Yusuf,
has so much to fill our lives.
A lesson in forgiveness and brotherhood we cannot compromise.
The power of patience and the fire of hope,
must burn in the hearts of the wise.
The beautiful story of Yusuf,
has so much to fill our lives.

It seemed like endless days and morningless nights,
his family so blind with concern,
while he held tight to his hope and his faith in Allah,
for the day they would see his return.
The guards laughing in the black of the night
as they kicked him and beat him raw;
the blood and the dirt and the grime of the world,
and the dark side of man that he saw.
And in the minutes and months and years that dripped by,
greying away his youth,
he spent his hours in quiet worship
and in silent *jihad* for the truth.

The beautiful story of Yusuf,
has so much to fill our lives.
A lesson in forgiveness and brotherhood we cannot compromise.
The power of patience and the fire of hope,
must burn in the hearts of the wise.
The beautiful story of Yusuf,
has so much to fill our lives.

He wiped tears from his cheek with the smile on his face,
brushed the hair back from his daughter's eyes,
and as she finished her lesson and closed her Qur'an,
it was clear then to recognize,
Allah only tests those Allah loves.
His little girl climbed up onto his knees.
The words of Allah are clear to the world,
'Along with hardship will always come ease.'

Oh, the beautiful story of Yusuf,
has so much to fill our lives.
A lesson in forgiveness and brotherhood we cannot compromise.
The power of patience and the fire of hope,
must burn in the hearts of the wise.
The beautiful story of Yusuf,
has so much to fill our lives.

Try a Little Little Bit

> If you try a little, little bit,
> that's all that you can do.
> When things get you up tight, bringing you down,
> try a little bit to turn 'em around,
> and try a little, little bit.
> That's the only thing that's best.
> 'Cause if you set your mind,
> you'll always find that God will do the rest.

When Moses was in Egypt, running from the Pharaoh,
he came up to the Red Sea, and there was nowhere else to go.
He had to find a way across and he had to make it quick,
then God inspired Moses to hit the water with a stick.

Moses hit that water just as hard a she could hit,
and he stood back from that seaside and he watched that water
    split.
Then Moses and his friends walked through to the other side.
They got away home free that day and all because they tried.

> If you try a little, little bit,
> that's all that you can do.
> When things get you up tight, bringing you down,
> try a little bit to turn 'em around,
> and try a little, little bit.
> That's the only thing that's best.
> 'Cause if you set your mind,
> you'll always find that God will do the rest.

When Mary, the mother of Jesus, was about to have her son,
she went out in the desert far away from everyone.
She was hot and tired and hungry from her *hijab* to her feet.
God guided her to shake a tree, so she'd find food to eat.

Mary placed her hands on the palm tree with a slap and a punch
    and a pound,
and suddenly ripe dates just started raining on the ground.

> Yes – she tried a little, little bit,
> that's all that you can do.
> When things get you up tight, bringing you down,
> try a little bit to turn 'em around,
> and try a little, little bit.
> That's the only thing that's best.
> 'Cause if you set your mind,
> you'll always find that God will do the rest.

The prophet Muhammad, heard an angel call his name,
giving him God's message saying, 'Read and proclaim!'
Muhammad he was shaken and he didn't think he knew,
how to do just what that angel was asking him to do.

Muhammad learned those words and taught them to his friends,
now we have the Qur'an to guide us all, 'till all time ends.

> If you try a little, little bit,
> that's all that you can do.
> When things get you up tight, bringing you down,
> try a little bit to turn 'em around,
> and try a little, little bit.
> That's the only thing that's best.
> 'Cause if you set your mind,
> you'll always find that God will do the rest.

Passion (Mark's Suicide at 3:43)

Now – as I sit here,
I can't think very clear.
My thoughts are cluttered,
and these last few years,
may have been a waste of my breath.

Now – as I pull myself up,
my thoughts are corrupt.
My feet and wrists are numb.
My head is heavy,
your eyes are cold on my naked skin and soul.

I thirst for knowledge and must know why,
before I die,
what have I done?
And for who?
My mother hides
and father has fled.

They don't understand I've tried –
and I know I've tried.
I forgive their ignorance.
It is over now.
It's finished.

I sit down.
I die.

The Old Fool

'Come watch me,' yelled the foolish old man, 'I have music to play for you!' Then he mimed out a flute, but the tune it was sweet and as real as you and me, and it carried away with the wind.

'Come watch me, and listen,' the old fool said, 'I'll tell you a tale to bring tears to your eyes!' He had no book or scrap of page but the story it flowed and it made us all weep.

'And watch me,' he yelled from the top of a cliff overlooking the valley at sunset, 'and I'll paint you a scene!' We all saw his painting of dusk with its trees and glowing sun – very real indeed – though he had not used a brush, nor canvas, nor paint.

Finally, he said to us all, 'Come and I'll show you life!' He began to dance and sing, so full of energy, we all began to do the same, one by one: we all came to life.

When the old fool saw this, he smiled and then he stole away to the forest, where he died.

Fi Qalbi (In My Heart)
(with thanks to Mohamed Benammi)

A carpenter of faith,
    tore down the old walls to build hearts strong.
A shepherd of the soul,
    freed his flock to guide them along.

I just can't understand,
    why we carve lines in the sand.
All the towers and walls we build,
    to hide the ghosts of hope we've killed.

About Muhammad

It would be such a pleasure to have you come along with me,
I accept your gracious offer of kindness and company.
But as we walk along young man and as you help me with my load,
I have only one request as we travel down this road.

Don't talk to me about Muhammad.
Because of him there is no peace and I have trouble in my mind.
So don't talk to me about Muhammad,
and as we walk along together we will get along just fine,
and as we walk along together we will get along.

That man upsets me so, and so much more than you could know,
I hear of his name and reputation everywhere I go.
Though his family and his clan once knew him as an honest man,
he's dividing everyone with his claim that 'God is One'.

So don't talk to me about Muhammad.
Because of him there is no peace and I have trouble in my mind.
So don't talk to me about Muhammad
and as we walk along together we will get along just fine,
and as we walk along together we will get along.

He's misled all the weak ones and the poor ones and the slaves,
they think they've all found wealth and freedom following his ways.
He's corrupted all the youth with his twisted brand of truth,
convinced them that they all are strong, given them somewhere
    to belong.

So don't talk to me about Muhammad.
Because of him there is no peace and I have trouble in my mind.
Don't talk to me about Muhammad,
and as we walk along together we will get along just fine,
and as we walk along together we will get along.

Thank you now young man, you've really been so kind,
your generosity and smile are very rare to find.
Let me give you some advice, since you've been so very nice,
From Muhammad stay away, don't heed his words or emulate
    his way,

and don't talk about Muhammad,
or you will never have true peace and trouble is all you will find.
So don't talk about Muhammad,
and as you travel down life's road you will get along just fine.

Now before we part and go, if it's alright just the same,
may I ask, my dear young man, who are you? What's your name?

Forgive me – what was that? Your words weren't very clear.
My ears are getting old – sometimes it's difficult to hear.
It's truly rather funny – though I'm sure I must be wrong –
but I thought I heard you said, your name was Muhammad...

Muhammad?

Ash hadu alla ilaha illallah wa ash hadu anna Muhammadur rasulullah.

Oh, talk to me Muhammad!
Upon you I pray for peace, for you have eased my troubled mind!
Oh, talk to me Muhammad!
And as we walk along together we will get along just fine.
As I travel down life's road I will get along just fine.

Madinatun Nabi

There was merriment and joy,
a smile on the face of every girl and boy.
The streets of Yathrib welcomed in
the prophet of Allah,
Muhammad,
Sallallahu 'alaihi was sallam.

A full, white moon,
shone down upon the land,
rising from the valley between hills of sand.
Being grateful to Allah was the prophet's demand,
spreading peace through the streets of Madinah.

> *Madinatun Nabi!*
> *Madinatun Nabi!*
> The city of the prophet is like home to me.
> I'll travel through the world but I doubt that I will see,
> a city with such wonder as Madinah.

Now the narrow winding roads,
are so full of history;
Streets shake with the *azan* from *Masjidun Nabi.*
I feel the shadow of the prophet gently cooling me,
as I walk through the streets of Madinah.

> *Madinatun Nabi!*
> *Madinatun Nabi!*
> The city of the prophet is like home to me.
> I'll travel through the world but I doubt that I will see,
> a city with such wonder as Madinah.

The man who reads Qur'an 'neath a date palm tree,
and the smile from a child on the street selling tea,
enchant me with their beauty and their simplicity,
as I walk through the streets of Madinah.

Al Madinatul Munawarah!
Oh, Enlightened City!
Al Madinatul Munawarah!
Even in my sleep you call to me.

Time, has hurried by, time has travelled on so fast,
and though wisdom and truth will always last,
I wish, I wish, I wish that I could climb into the past,
and live with the prophet in Madinah.

> *Madinatun Nabi*!
> *Madinatun Nabi*!
> The city of the prophet is like home to me.
> I'll travel through the world but I doubt that I will see,
> a city with such wonder as Madinah.

My heart is never far from the home of the *Ansar*,
and the city of the prophet, *Al Madinah*.

The Prophet

Muhammad, *'alaihis salam*,
sat quietly in the evening.
His companion asked,
'Oh beautiful man, why do you sit here, grieving?'

'My *ummah*, those who follow me,
the future of their faith makes me worry 'til I cry.
My brothers and sisters in *islam*,
will they be strong and carry on after I die?'

The prophet stood silently and prayed,
his beard becoming wet as he cried for his fears.
'Oh Allah, don't let this nation fade!'
As he pleaded through the night,
the earth around him filled with tears.

'My *ummah*, those who follow me,
the future of their faith makes me worry 'til I cry.
My brothers and sisters in *islam*,
will they be strong and carry on after I die?'

As stillness fell over the land.
Companions gathered near to where the prophet lay.
As Ayesha, his wife, held tightly to his hand,
the prophet spoke again before he passed away,

'My *ummah*, those who follow me,
the future of their faith makes me worry 'til I cry.
My brothers and sisters in *islam*,
will they be strong and carry on after I die?'

Believers,
brothers and sisters in *islam*,
will we be strong and carry on until we die?

Sunshine Dust and the Messenger

Morning light through the bedroom window.
Slow motion dust specks swirling in the sun.
I close my eyes and I'm floating along.
Sun – did you warm the face of the prophet,
the way you warm mine and make this room glow?
Dust – were you brushed from the beard of the prophet,
returning from *jihad*, so long ago?

Allahumma salli 'ala Muhammad. Ya Rabbal 'alamin!
Allahumma salli 'ala Muhammad, sallallahu 'alaihi wa sallam.

Rain pouring down upon my garden,
rhythm for the wind that sings her song.
I close my eyes and I'm drumming along.
Rhythm of rain – were you once a river,
that purified the prophet before his prayers?
Wind – were you a breath form the lips of the prophet,
carrying wisdom to thirsty ears?

Allahumma salli 'ala Muhammad. Ya Rabbal 'alamin!
Allahumma salli 'ala Muhammad, sallallahu 'alaihi wa sallam.

Sharp clear crescent, light in the blue night,
slipping in silence through a star scattered sky.
I close my eyes and I know that I belong.
Were you the same moon that lit the way of the prophet,
slipping through the desert on his *hijrah*?
Stars did you map the way to Madinah,
for the blessed messenger of Allah?

Allahumma salli 'ala Muhammad. Ya Rabbal 'alamin!
Allahumma salli 'ala Muhammad, sallallahu 'alaihi wa sallam.

I close my eyes,
and I'm floating along.   (*salam*!)
I close my eyes   (*sallallahu 'alaihi*
and I'm drumming a song.   *wa sallam*!)

I close my eyes
and I know that I belong.

PART IV

FOR THE FAITHFUL

Blind Faith

He folds his hands in prayer,
and gently closes his eyes.
His lips move quickly in quiet recital.
He does not know who he prays to,
nor why.

Yet he does,
lest he be struck down tomorrow.

Out Seeing the Fields

Briskly, rising to the sky.
Cold, clouds rushing past.
Flying, hopes to never land.
Light. Stretching out my hand.

> Out seeing the fields.
> What is a dream and can you tell me what is real?
> Everyone else is home in bed,
> and I'm out here lost in my own head.
> Out seeing the fields.

Freeze, crystal on the bridge.
Trees. Frozen diamond leaves.
Ice, stiffening the wheat.
Wind, underneath my feet.

> Out seeing the fields.
> What is a dream and can you tell me what is real?
> Everyone else is home in bed,
> and I'm out here lost in my own head.
> Out seeing the fields.

I only feel close to you when I'm under open sky.
I only feel guided when I'm free to question why.
Only when I smell the earth upon my face,
will I ever be free to fly from this place.
Out seeing the fields.

> Leaving the place I thought was home before.
> Picking up my shoes and I'm flying out the door.
> Can't seem to want to go back there anymore,
> so I'm out seeing the fields.

Morning, wings against the ledge.
Frost, trees painted on the glass.
Snow, covering the streets.
Home, warm beneath the sheets.

Al Khaliq

> *La ilaha illallah,*
> *Muhammadur rasulullah,*
> *sallallahu ʿalaihi was sallam!*

Al Khaliq made the oceans,
rivers, lakes, streams, and rain,
bow their waves in pure submission,
upon the earth to praise God's name.

> *La ilaha illallah,*
> *Muhammadur rasulullah,*
> *sallallahu ʿalaihi was sallam!*

There is no creature among us,
upon the air or in the sea,
that does not sing with wonder,
praising in community.

La ilaha illallah,
Muhammadur rasulullah,
sallallahu 'alaihi was sallam!

The dry earth is a sign,
to all of mankind,
brought to life with peaceful rain,
and to us, Allah will do the same.

La ilaha illallah,
Muhammadur rasulullah,
sallallahu 'alaihi was sallam!

Allah Ta'ala

Everything Allah commands to be,
will always become a reality.
Allah Ta'ala!

You can try to hold back the waves,
but they will always wash upon your feet.
Two waters flow with a barrier in between,
the salty sea and rivers fresh and sweet.

Everything Allah commands to be,
will always become a reality.
Allah Ta'ala!

Every leaf that falls off every tree,
and settles to the ground so far below,
only breaks away and sails on a breeze,
when Allah commands it to do so.

Everything Allah commands to be,
will always become a reality.
Allah Ta'ala!

We can try to sew a seed,
so deep and dark within the ground.
Plant it, pat it, scare off every weed,
but no matter how long we wait around,
we can never make it grow, you know,
unless Allah commands it so.

> Everything Allah commands to be,
> will always become a reality.
> *Allah Ta'ala*!

Even Animals Love Qur'an

There was a chipmunk climbing up a tree,
I stopped to look at him and he stopped to look at me.
When I said 'hello', he didn't understand and he went to run away,
I recited from Qur'an and he decided to stay.

> Animals love to hear Qur'an, try it out some day,
> they'll stop to listen carefully to every word you say.
> Allah created animals, Allah created man,
> and sent a book to guide us all, even animals love Qur'an.

Sitting at the window to ponder at the sky,
I saw a little bird as it flew by.
I recited from Qur'an and it wasn't very long,
'til the bird sat near my window and it started to sing along.

> Animals love to hear Qur'an, try it out some day,
> they'll stop to listen carefully to every word you say.
> Allah made the chipmunks and the birds, Allah
>   created man,
> and sent a book to guide us all, even animals love Qur'an.

Playing in the yard on a warm, sunny day
a shy little kitten watched me play.
I bent down to pat him on the head but I think he was scared of me,
I recited from Qur'an, he smiled and brushed against my knee.

> Animals love to hear Qur'an, try it out some day,
> they'll stop to listen carefully to every word you say.
> Allah made the chipmunks, birds and cats, Allah
>   created man,
> and sent a book to guide us all, even animals love Qur'an.
> Allah created animals, Allah is *Ar Rahman*,
> who sent a book to guide us all,
> even animals love Qur'an.

A Whisper of Peace

A whisper of peace,
moving through the land,
Allah will surely run to us
if we hold out our hand.
A word of hope,
a call to every woman and man,
a light until the end of time,
this is *al islam*.

A smile of hope,
spreading to each face,
a charity – like moonlight –
guiding all our human race.
A universal song,
to pass on while we're keeping pace.
A blessing without barrier,
and a gift of gentle grace.

Alhamdulillah (I'm a Rock)

I am just a rock and everyday I sit and watch the sky.
I sleep here in the sun and rain and do not question why.
I don't want to be a bird 'cause us rocks were never meant to fly.
But you can sit and rest on me when you pass by.

Alhamdulillah, alhamdulillah, I'm a rock,
and that is all Allah asks of me.
Alhamdulillah, alhamdulillah, I'm a *muslim*,
and there's nothing else I'd rather be.

I am just a tree and this is the only life I'll ever know.
I bow my boughs in worship whenever I feel the wind blow,
and my purpose in life is to grow when Allah says grow,
and be a home for the birds and shade for folks below.

Alhamdulillah, alhamdulillah, I'm a tree,
and that is all Allah asks of me.
Alhamdulillah, alhamdulillah, I'm a *muslim*,
and there's nothing else I'd rather be.

I am just a person and my life is full of opportunity.
I can travel through the world over land and over sea.
But will I choose the path of truth or a path to misguide me?
Sometimes I wish I had a simple life just like a rock or a tree.

But *alhamdulillah, alhamdulillah*, I'm a person,
and Allah has given me a choice that's free.
So, *alhamdulillah*, I choose to be a *muslim*,
and there's nothing else I'd rather be.

Vacuous Waxing
(written with Bill Kocher)

All the documents that insulate a cluttered shelf.
All the vacuous waxing history of myself.
All the analytical in depth study – when will it end?
I am my worst and I am my very best friend.
But all I want to think about is you.

Hearts so full of so much to say,
couldn't get it all out if we tried anyway.
With every ocean ink and every tree a pen,
how can so many illiterate souls give up on themselves each day?
And all I want to think about is you.

I want to start a sentence without the words 'I want',
to write a line without the words 'me', 'myself' or 'I' in it.
You can show me how I see my mirror-self absorbed,
with all the vacuous waxing history sent overboard.
But all I want to think about is you.

Remember Allah

You can always tell when Allah remembers you,
just remember Allah, that's all you have to do.
All you have to do to have Allah remember you,
is just remember Allah, *jala jalaluhu*.

Remember when you're swinging,
remember when you're singing,
remember when you're biking,
or hiking through the trees.
Remember when you're laughing,
remember when you're crying,
remember when you're working
in the garden on your knees!

You can always tell when Allah remembers you,
just remember Allah, that's all you have to do.
All you have to do to have Allah remember you,
is just remember Allah, *jalla jalaluhu*.

Make *zikr* when you're playing,
and *zikr* when you're praying.
Make *zikr* when you're walking
or standing in a line.
Make *zikr* in your head,
or when you're laying on your bed.
Make *zikr* in a chair,
make *zikr* anywhere!

You can always tell when Allah remembers you,
just remember Allah, that's all you have to do.
All you have to do to have Allah remember you,
is just remember Allah, *jalla jalaluhu*.

Your *zikr* is reflection,
that brings Allah's protection,
puts you in the right direction to love Allah!

You can always tell when Allah remembers you,
just remember Allah, that's all you have to do.
All you have to do to have Allah remember you,
is just remember Allah, *jalla jalaluhu*.

Truth that Lies Inside

You smile in the two-way mirror of my eyes,
I put on my faith like I wear a disguise.
You can't see my soul, see the life that I live.
I show you the mask of the best I can give.
I've hid here, afraid, like a child behind,
the truth of thoughts that clutter my mind.
What if you knew, about all that I do?
The things that I think, the 'me' that is true?

Would you call me a hypocrite?
Call me a liar?
Would you curse out my name?
Would you damn me to fire?
Would you know what to say?
Would you just walk away,
afraid that the 'me' I've tried to hide,
would too closely resemble
the truth of you that lies inside?

I've been looking for answers since becoming adult,
not looking for dogma to live like a cult.
I've been looking to live, I've been living to find,
freedom from cages that limit my mind.

Would you call me a hypocrite?
Call me a liar?
Would you curse out my name?
Would you damn me to fire?
Would you know what to say?
Would you just walk away,
afraid that the 'me' I've tried to hide,
would too closely resemble
the truth of you that lies inside?

I've been running and hiking and dreaming of flying,
but falling and stumbling never shadowed my trying.
So now here I am, before God and you,
showing my face and a self that is true.
I'm not sacred of God, I trust God understands,
but I'm wandering if you will still offer your hands?

Will I scare you? Frustrate you? Upset you? Irritate you?
Challenge your lifestyle or weaken your trust?
Or will you see my effort? My passion? Sincerity?
Will you see just a little of yourself in me?
Will you take off your mask so we can be free?

Would you call me a hypocrite?
Call me a liar?
Would you curse out my name?
Would you damn me to fire?
Would you know what to say?
Would you just walk away,
afraid that the 'me' I've tried to hide,
would too closely resemble
the truth of you that lies inside?

Would too closely resemble
the truth of you that lies?

Wings Against My Window
(with thanks to Abdul Malik Mujahid)

> Wings against my window,
> are they birds or are they angels,
> waking me for worship
> at *fajr* before dawn?
> Wings against my window,
> are they birds or are they angels,
> singing me from slumber?
> Soon night will be gone.

I hear sparrows whistle, making the *azan*.
I hear their words telling me I am a lazy man.
'Come fast to pray', they say,
'You will find success that way.
Stand up now from where you lay.
This is the best time of the day.'

> Wings against my window,
> are they birds or are they angels,
> waking me for worship
> at *fajr* before dawn?
> Wings against my window,
> are they birds or are they angels,
> singing me from slumber?
> Soon night will be gone.

My heart, it wants to wake up. My body wants to sleep.
The morning air is brisk and cool. My bed is warm and deep.
Birds, they call me to the way,
'Stand before Allah to pray!
Kiss the dawn and greet the day!'
But dreams, they just get in the way.

Wings against my window,
are they birds or are they angels,
waking me for worship
at *fajr* before dawn?
Wings against my window,
are they birds or are they angels,
singing me from slumber?
Soon night will be gone.

Qad Qamatis Salah

Wake up from your sleeping, say '*Bismillah*' as you rise.
Wake up from your dreaming, make *wudu* and rub your eyes.
As the darkness turns into the dawn, pray *fajr* to Allah.
As the moon cracks into daylight, sing '*Hayya 'alas salah*'.

Allahu akbar, Allahu ahad.
La ilaha illallah, hayya 'alas salah.

The burning sun begins to fall the second time we pray.
We turn our faces and our thoughts, to Allah at midday.
Food, it keeps our bodies strong, a blessing from Allah.
'Ibadah feeds our spirit, sing '*Hayya 'alal falah*'.
Allahu akbar, Allahu ahad
La ilaha illallah, hayya 'alal falah.

Some of us, we race with time, we always lose the run,
for time is always keeping with the passing of the sun.
But we'll be straight upon our way if we bow to pray throughout
     the day,
taking time for *'Asr* from our afternoon of play.

Allahu akbar, Allahu ahad
La ilaha illallah, hayya 'alas salah.
Allahu akbar, Allahu ahad
La ilaha illallah, hayya 'alal falah.
Allahu akbar, Allahu ahad
La ilaha illallah, qad qamatis salah.

As daytime drips away, the setting of the day,
we turn our faces to Allah, at *Maghrib* time we bow to pray.
And when the sky is black, the moon awake so steep,
we pray the *'Isha* for Allah before we go to sleep.

Allahu akbar, Allahu ahad
La ilaha illallah, hayya 'alas salah.
Allahu akbar, Allahu ahad
La ilaha illallah, hayya 'alal falah.
Allahu akbar, Allahu ahad
La ilaha illallah, qad qamatis salah.

All the Crazy Spots I've Prayed

> All the earth is a place of prostration,
> every field and meadow, mountain, park, city,
>   farm, plantation.
> Every roadside, seaside, hillside, walk way,
> any place clean and green can be a place to pray.
> When I think of every path, where I have ever trod,
> I laugh at all the crazy spots I've stopped to worship God.

Remember that long car ride?
Driving all night so far?
Under the summer moon we pulled of to the side,
reclining in the front seat of the car.
Waking to a *fajr* bird's sound,
and washing in the coin carwash we found
with a water blaster making *wudu*,
you sprayed me and I sprayed you.
We stood so drowsy in with dawn,
behind the carwash, drippin' on the lawn.

> All the earth is a place of prostration,
> every field and meadow, mountain, park, city,
>   farm, plantation.
> Every roadside, seaside, hillside, walk way,
> any place clean and green can be a place to pray.
> When I think of every path, where I have ever trod,
> I laugh at all the crazy spots I've stopped to worship God.

Saturday shopping day,
bustling busy mall, I'm busting through the aisles.
Worldly wants gettin' in my way.
Each blank zombie shopper face void of smiles.
Time comes for a prayer attack,
grab a pair of pants or a sweater from a rack,
find a change room and latch the door,
set aside excuses and hit the floor.
As I go back to the mall,
it's easier then to make sense of it all.

> All the earth is a place of prostration,
> every field and meadow, mountain, park, city,
>   farm, plantation.
> Every roadside, seaside, hillside, walk way,
> any place clean and green can be a place to pray.
> When I think of every path, where I have ever trod,
> I laugh at all the crazy spots I've stopped to worship God.

Our socks froze to the blanket that we spread over the snow,
your call to prayer bounced off the trees and across the icy meadow.
Crisp and clean cold air, our hearts were so aware.
Our bodies felt the frozen freedom.
What a very cool place for prayer.

There was the time next to the river,
there was the time in the school hall,
there was the stairwell in the that building,
there was that forest in the fall,
the movie house corridor,
the air-plane kitchen in the sky,
so many places and I'm sure there'll be more
pieces of earth to testify.

> All the earth is a place of prostration,
> every field and meadow, mountain, park, city,
>   farm, plantation.
> Every roadside, seaside, hillside, walk-way,
> any place clean and green can be a place to pray.
> When I think of every path, where I have ever trod,
> I laugh at all the crazy spots I've stopped to worship God.

What Did I Do Today?

Oh, the moon has come, the day is done,
the night has covered up the sun,
I have stood so often before you to pray,
but I wonder Allah, tell me, what did I do today?
Did I remember the words of *Al Fatiha*?
Did I take time to thank you for all that I have?
Did I call on you to guide my way?
Tell me what did I do today?

I have whispered to you as I made *ruku*
'Subhana Rabbiyal 'azim.'
But was my faith bright or grey?
Oh Allah, tell me, what did I do today?
Did I smile at my brother?
Was I kind to my mother?
Did I teach another something that I know,
or did my love of this world lead me astray?
Tell me what did I do today?

Sami Allahu liman hamidah,
Rabbana lakal hamd.
La ilaha ilallah, Allah!

Though I've bowed to you with my face in the dust,
'Subhana Rabbiyal a'la.'
The blessings you give I could never repay.
Oh Allah, tell me, what did I do today?
Did I use my time?
Did I use my mind?
If I search my heart what will I find?
The light of your guidance is a glimmering ray,
tell me, what did I do today?

Oh Allah, tell me what did I do today?

Lullaby

In your name, Oh Lord, I lay to sleep,
      to rise in the morning, by your leave.
If you take my soul from me as I rest,
      please forgive me.
And if I wake in the morning again,
      to a new and bright day,
then I pray you will always guide me
      upon the straight way.

Here We Come

Here we come, Allah!
Here we come to serve you!
Here we come, no partner do you have!
All praise to you!
The universe is yours!
Here we come, Allah!
Here we come!

The world is a very, very big house,
many people, living in many rooms.
We must open all the doors up.
We must unlock them all today,
throw all the keys away.

Here we come, Allah!
Here we come to serve you!
Here we come, no partner do you have!
All praise to you!
The universe is yours!
Here we come, Allah!
Here we come!

Oceans and mountains divide us,
but the same fire burns inside us.
We must throw the world behind us.
With Allah is where you'll find us – here.
Here we come, oh, here!

Here we come, Allah!
Here we come to serve you!
Here we come, no partner do you have!
All praise to you!
The universe is yours!
Here we come, Allah!
Here we come!

We've Scanned the Sky (The Ramadan Song)

> We've scanned the sky and we've sighted the moon,
> and we welcome the month of Ramadan.
> When we'll fast together, all as one,
> to help and strengthen our *iman*.

Oh, it was so very long ago, in the holy month of Ramadan.
Allah sent a message to the world, the holy book of Qur'an.
A light to shine for all mankind, a guide to teach us right from
   wrong.
First revealed on the night of power, with peace until the rising of
   the dawn.

> We've scanned the sky and we've sighted the moon,
> and we welcome the month of Ramadan.
> When we'll fast together, all as one,
> to help and strengthen our *iman*.

As the sun lay sleeping, beneath the blanket of the night,
we rise early to make *suhur*, before the white thread of light.
We're patient and kind, remembering Allah,
all throughout our day,
when the sun has gone and we've made *iftar*,
we bow together and pray.

> 'Cause we've scanned the sky and we've sighted the moon,
> and we welcome the month of Ramadan.
> When we'll fast together, all as one,
> to help and strengthen our *iman*.

So many of our brothers and sisters, all across the land,
they have no food to eat at all and they need a helping hand.
When we fast from morning 'til the night, to fulfil Allah's
    command,
we feel the hunger and thirst they feel, and it helps us to
    understand.

But all too fast, the moon goes past, our month of blessings now
    has gone.
We must keep its spirit throughout the year, everyday should be
    like Ramadan.

> We've scanned the sky and we've sighted the moon
> and we say 'Farewell' to Ramadan,
> when we fast together, all as one,
> to help and strengthen our *iman*.

Hear Me Beat My Drum

The rhythm of your breathing is so soft,
as you lay up in your beds so sweetly dreaming.
Through your windows, smells of bread and sounds of drumming
    drift and waft,
to fill your nose and ear,
and tell you that the dawn is near.

Wrapped up like baked pastries in your sheets,
I know you're tucked away so warm and cozy.
There's tea and dates and sweets, a *suhur* party in the streets,
so get up out of bed!
Come and greet the day ahead!

> Hear me beat my drum, as down your street I come.
> The moon is falling, I am calling,
> to wake you for the day that's on her way.
> Get yourselves out of bed, before the night is gone,
> to welcome a new day of Ramadan.

Our busy little lives can make us crazy,
and it's so easy to get stuck in a routine.
Doing everything the same way everyday can make us lazy,
so let's take control today,
live our lives in a new way.

So wake up! Stop you're dreaming.
Let us wake the neighbourhood,
to share in all that's good, the pots of *ful* are steaming,
let's break our dull routine,
let all the world join in the scene.

> Hear me beat my drum,
> as down your street I come.
> The moon is falling, I am calling,
> to wake you for the day that's on her way.
> Get yourselves out of bed, before the night is gone,
> to welcome a new day of Ramadan.

A Whisper of Peace (Reprise)

A whisper of peace,
moving through the land,
Allah will surely run to us if we hold out our hand.
A word of hope, a call to every woman and man,
a light until the end of time,
this is *al islam*.

A whisper of peace,
moving through the land,
Allah will surely run to us but do we understand?
A word of hope a call to every woman and man,
a light until the end of time...

or is this just a waste of rhyme?

What if we run out of time?

Is this our *islam*?

PART V

FOR THE KING'S COURT

Wood and Nails

Build me a tomb for when I die.
Build it fifty thousand feet into the sky.
I am the king do as I say.
I want to see the moon resting upon its pinnacle.
We'll never run out of wood and nails.

Build me a boat I want to discover America (Land of the Free).
Build me a boat to take me to the edge of the seven seas.
Build me a boat, and you can sail along with me.
We'll spread our money, power, religion and disease. ('In God
    we trust')
We'll never run out of wood and nails.

You've built me a cabin but I want more and more and more.
Build me an office tower with an automatic door.
Build me a fence that I can wrap around my state.
If anyone tries to break through, I pity his fate.
We'll never run out of wood and nails.

Who are they to say
that we own nothing and our lives have gone astray?
We have dealt with all these idealists in the past
                (Martin Luther King, Malcolm X, Gandhi, J.F.K.)
I'm sure we'll find a way to deal with them today.
Rid our world of these fanatics one by one.
                        (We'll string 'em up and shoot 'em down!)
Won't let no prophet lover ruin my fun.
We'll never run out of wood and nails.

Ya Ummati

(written with Jen Zaghloul and Asifa Sheikh,
dedicated to Farah Khan)

Come listen to her story with me,
in a world of opportunity.
A little girl has lots to say,
but everyone's so far away.
Come listen to her story with me.
Her tiny life and tiny hands shake,
ashamed of her unknown mistake.
A child's hopes and tears in vain,
she believes she is to blame.
Listen to her story with me.

> '*Ya ummati* answer me, why am I suffering this way?
> *Ummati* I am so afraid. Don't I have the right to learn
> and play?'

A silent call to you and to me.
Too caught up with our lives to hear or see.
We will answer to Allah one day,
then what will we have to say
for busy lives so void of mercy?

> '*Ya ummati* answer me, why am I suffering this way?
> *Ummati* I am so afraid. Don't I have the right to learn
> and play?'

Allah created beauty, innocence and peace,
and blessed us with the children to remind us all of these.
Allah entrusted to us all a gift to hold so near:
To teach with love – teach how to love – Allah's command is clear.
In Allah's garden there's a flower at play,
the abandoned gift we turned away.
Had we only been brave enough to hear,
her playground prayer to our deaf ear,
her smile might not haunt us today.

'*Ya ummati* answer me, why am I suffering this way?
Ummati I am so afraid. Don't I have the right to learn
      and play?'

Ummati we all know the answer.
The ignorance must end today.
Ummati open your heart.
Every child has the right to learn and play.
Every child has the right to grow and pray.
Every child has a right.

Twinkle, Twinkle

Twinkle, twinkle satellite,
      shining like a star so bright.

Cluttering up the evening sky.
      You're not a star you are a lie.

Twinkle, twinkle satellite.
      Man-made garbage in the night.

The War / La ilaha iIlallah

Turn our faces to our Makkah,
of the markets before dawn.
Our profit speaks to us,
counted once the sun is gone.
What do we hope to gain?
Work our hands and spirits raw?
La ilaha illallah, Muhammadur rasulullah.

Teachers and pop icons,
empty drums beat loudest noise.
We swap their quotes and CDs,
like children trading toys.
Follow along,
bite the barbed hook in our jaw,
La ilaha illallah, Muhammadur rasulullah.

Pictures of politicians,
preen across our TV screens.
Pretentious plaques and posters,
stain our minds and magazines
Promises a burning match,
igniting dreams of straw,
La ilaha illallah, Muhammadur rasulullah.

I glance reflections of my face
everyplace I go,
in my mirror and in shop windows,
like the lead in my own show.
Do I dare look closely?
See each wrinkle, scar and flaw?
La ilaha illallah, Muhammadur rasulullah.

Prophet for Profit

You're reading from the scriptures again,
election poles, collection plates and pockets padded again.
In your rigid mind, hide all the rules that you bend.
We're either with you or against you, well we'll see in the end.

> Don't think you lead me,
> as you lead yourself on, with the lines that you speak.
> And don't think you fool me.
> Behind your prophet's beard,
> there's a profit you seek.

Papa Arrogant Smurf smirk on my TV screen,
When you say, 'God bless us', I know what you mean.
The rockets red glare, the bombs bursting in air,
under your colourful smoke, your cartoon world's a joke.

     ·   Don't think you lead me,
          as you lead yourself on with the lies that you speak.
          Don't think you fool me.
          Behind the dunes that you search,
          there's a profit you seek.

Behind the passion I hold there are millions like me,
deaf to your definitions of democracy,
and we don't want your twisted spirituality,
and we don't want your bloody hands on the scriptures we read.

Freedom is a word that we've all over-heard,
in this holy war crusade where rhetoric is absurd.
Where faith and state join to dictate fate,
and 'freedom' means 'free to dominate'.

          Don't think you lead me,
          as you lead yourself on, with the lines that you speak.
          Don't think you fool me.
          Behind your prophet's beard there is a profit you seek.
          Behind the dunes that you search, there's a profit you seek.
          Behind the cities you free, there is an oil leak.
          Behind your prophet's beard you're a coward who's weak.
          Beyond the city's debris, there is the bed where you sleep
              in peace.
          How can you rest in peace?

Welcome to the I.C.E.

This is America, land of the free,
where everyone is given equal opportunity.
A living dream, a land of plenty, milk and honey, neon lights,
but once you step inside these doors, my friend, you don't hold
    any rights.
So go and sit down there and obediently wait your turn,
get familiar with your chair and watch your time and patience
    burn,

      and welcome to the I.C.E.
      How long you'll be here, well it's all up to me,
      'cause we're working in conjunction with Homeland Security,
      so while you're in this country we'll decide if you are free.

Your name shows up here in our highlighted file,
says your ex-wife's cousin's husband lived in Baghdad for a while.
Says your uncle's neighbour's father's brother-in-law's
    nephew's twin,
delivered groceries to man who looked a lot like Bin Laden.
Though that's as close as we can get, we're almost sure that you're
    a threat.
Everybody must be checked,
each beard and headscarf is suspect.

      Welcome to the I.C.E.
      How long you'll be here, well, we'll have to wait and see,
      'cause we're working in conjunction with Homeland Security,
      so while you're in this country we'll decide if you are free.

Though we can't pronounce your name, let alone correctly spell it,
if there's a terrorist, fundo, suspect rat our nose is trained to
    smell it.
So don't ask why or try to lie.
When we say 'jump' just ask 'how high'.
Don't underestimate our pomp, prestige or our power,
We're the highest-paid government pawns at $25 bucks an hour.

Yes, this here is a modern-day crusade.
You're either with us...or you're with the Moslems...er...I mean
    the 'terrorists'.
We're gonna route you out, we're gonna smoke you out,
we're gonna shine a light on ya!

So you're old, withered, white haired, blind and you need
    a wheel chair,
so you're almost eight months pregnant – well we don't really care.
Just get up! Faster! Face your luggage! Hands outstretched
    arms high!
We'll pat you down and feel you up and it's treason to ask why.
Just democratically comply.

        And welcome to the I.C.E.
        How long you'll be here, well it's all up to me,
        'cause we're working in conjunction with Homeland Security,
        so while you're in this country we'll decide if you are free.

In this land of the free,
your fate belongs to me.
In the name of freedom,
we'll destroy what it means to be free.

What Has Become (with thanks to Sami Yusuf)

I must be a backward man –
torn-out values, wear and fray.
Hues of coloured dreams you paint,
blend and mix to me as grey.
All the reds and whites and blues,
options you dictate as true,
leave me only with a choice to
fade away or be like you.

> What has become of self-respect? Freedom to
>   choose or to reject?
> What has become of dignity? The right to hold identity?
> What of wars we have survived? Holocausts and genocides?
> Have our hopes for humankind, like scriptures
>   and mass graves – been lost?

> Your bombs and pens like swords, held high, up to
>   my throat.
> You have made the cost of blood, as cheap as ink
>   and all I think.
> *Ya Allah*!

If a fist can hold a sword,
and a fist can clench a pen,
but the points of both are missed,
by dull, tarnished pride of men.
We must open up our hands,
raise our palms up high to see,
the mazes of our unique selves,
end with similarity.

What has become of self-respect? Freedom to
    choose or to reject?
What has become of dignity? The right to hold identity?
Who is this god whom we command, to bless
    our coloured flag and land?
So busy drawing lines in sand that we don't read
    and understand.

And if we only knew, the sacred value,
of human life and faith, could we draw with such disgrace?

And if the might of our pen, is stronger than the
    swords of men,
let us unsheathe our minds, write with our hearts again.
Ya Allah!

Why Are the Drums So Silent?

All the sounds that surround us,
all the noises that dumbfound us,
the clatter and the clamour of the clutter of our lives.
Cars and streets make silence shatter,
idle minds fill up with idle chatter,
if we fill our void that's all that matters.

    Why are the drums so silent?
    Why can't we hear the rhythm? What's wrong
        with you and I?
    Why are the drums so silent?
    Why can't we hear the rhythm from the heels of believers
    marching to the garden as they strive?

We've digitized The Revelation,
but does our rehearsed recitation
go any deeper than our throats?
Our calls to prayer seem to rise up to the sky,
conferences and lectures, seminars for you and I,
the words that blow away with *anashid* that make us cry yet,

> why are the drums so silent?
> Why can't we hear the rhythm? What's wrong
>   with you and I?
> Why are the drums so silent?
> Why can't we hear the rhythm from the heels of believers
> marching to the garden as they strive?

If we can just be brave enough to be each other's mirror,
we may finally recognize the face of conscience that we fear.
And if we take the time to mute the noise we've built around
   ourselves,
the rhythm of the heartbeats and the purpose may be clear,

If we beat the drum.... (a whisper of peace?)
Beat the drum...   (moving through the land)

> If we beat the drums of hope and faith,
> we will all fall into rhythm, I have faith in you and I.
> If we beat the drums of hope and faith, then we will
>   feel the rhythm
> from our footsteps and our striving,
> marching to the garden as we try.

> Marching to the garden as we die.

Song of Freedom

There is a song I have been meaning to write about freedom,
a poem I have been meaning to pen about innocence,
a script that needs to be started about truth and justice,
a novel about forgiveness,
a letter of love.
There is a treaty that must be signed about peace.

This is the song.
This is the poem.
This is the script,
the novel,
the letter of love.

This is an effort,
        and we must fight,
        and we must write
        until our swords run out of ink.

Sign your name here,

        for this is the treaty of peace.

Reflections

As a young man engaged in the discipline of keeping a written journal, the discovery of poetry came almost by accident. Thoughts and reflections were quickly jotted down in a crude and abstract fashion, as a way of documenting my sentiments and daily experiences. Upon re-reading these notes, re-examining them beyond the context of dated diary entries, some of them revealed themselves as poignant paintings of words – poems, songs and short stories – capturing distinct emotions or moments in time. A lover of songs since childhood and a student of vocal music throughout my teens, melody has always underscored my thoughts. During the process of revisiting my journal entries and snippets of often unintentional poetry, the words would unconsciously begin to fall together musically in my mind.

Early attempts at sharing my poetry with others through simple, self-published books were expensive and ineffective. It became evident to me that wider audiences for my work could perhaps be found if the writings were recorded with their accompanying melodies and released as songs. Taking cues from other Canadian poets and storytellers whose words went beyond the page and into the medium of music, I recorded my first album of original songs in 1995 entitled *Blue Walls and the Big Sky*.

Live performances provided me with platforms to share my very personal writings, but nightclubs and bar scenes proved to be ill-fitting venues for my style of intimate and introspective music. Even folk festival crowds seemed to politely endure my acoustic journal entries while waiting for the next artist's Celtic reel or familiar Irish ballad. Audiences were hearing me and were gracious with their applause – but I sensed they may not have really been listening.

I decided upon an alternative approach and took my music out onto the streets, hoping that those who were truly interested in my work would find their way to me. In true troubadour fashion, I began to combine my poems, melodies and stories with the business of peddling my songs from town to town as a street busker, seeking inspiration for further music along the way.

Families stopped and listened, sending toddlers bravely toward me to place coins in my guitar case. Frequently, other young travellers loitered within earshot, tossing smiles, loose change or their own homemade demo cassettes my way before moving on. Children, passing in packs, expressed approval with hoots and applause, or spat at me and ran away. Occasionally, new mothers with napping infants sat on nearby benches, closed their eyes and briefly escaped into the songs I played. Generally though, it was the homeless, unwell, elderly, lonely or troubled who would stand nearby, urging me to keep singing.

A gradual evolution toward more spiritually-centred lyrics, often written as educational refrains for youth, welcomed more interest from new audiences internationally. Teachers were suddenly inviting me to their schools, social activists requested my participation in their rallies, and clergy of various faith communities welcomed me to sing at their meetings of prayer or meditation. Communities of adults with disabilities, charities raising funds for positive social efforts, city counsel representatives or mayors hosting events to promote social cohesion – all began calling upon me to share in their gatherings. With a guitar case in one hand and a suitcase in the other, I have found homes for my songs in tents, town halls, hotels, houses, community centres, classrooms, libraries and parks.

For Whom the Troubadour Sings contains approximately half of my completed poetry, written between 1989 and 2009. Each writing within this particular anthology fits neatly alongside its own accompanying melody (the only exception being the last entry, the ironically titled 'Song of Freedom') and most have been released publicly over the years as recordings in various musical styles. Those who have heard and supported my music will note many unfamiliar titles listed in the contents of this collection – songs that have never before been captured in a studio or performed live.

French linguists often suggest the origin of the word 'troubadour' rests in the Occitan word *trobador*, meaning 'finder' or 'one who finds after searching'. Some linguists, however, trace the root for 'troubadour' to the Arabic word *tarrab*, meaning 'to sing'. While compiling this anthology, I began to reflect upon my collected writings, my excessive travel and how my personal search for answers to life's oldest questions has permeated the majority of my poetry. I began to wonder: What have I been seeking? What have I found along the way thus far? Who are my travel companions and audiences? For whom do *I* write? For whom do I *truly* sing?

Upon a closer study of my writings, themes addressing five common aspects of life emerged. This anthology has thus, been divided into five sections, each representing a specific 'environment' where I, as the travelling troubadour, often find myself singing, or the 'audiences' to whom my words are often addressed.

Part I, or 'The Journey', holds the largest and most diverse number of songs. These are the airs reflecting the most common aspects of 'the human experience' between birth and death. The words honour our shared joys and struggles with growth, choices, change, fear, anger, love and loss.

In Part II, the songs 'to inspire' are poems aimed at motivating us toward positive social action. These compositions – many of which were initially written for children – constantly touch on how our behaviour directly effects those around us. They also urge young and old alike to be conscious of their surroundings and environments, and to make efforts to build relationships and improve communities.

In our desire to move forward with hope and optimism for our world, it is important that we take time to look back with humility at where we have come from as a human family. Songs documenting history, myth or the wisdom of the ancients have always been a part of folk music, contained within the travelling minstrel's repertoire. In Part III, offerings I have written 'to remind' myself and others of the struggles and successes past prophets and peoples have endured are also designed to remind us of who we are now. Transcending the past and present, a fable like 'The People of the Boxes' acts as a warning of where we could end up, if we do not avoid the pitfalls that consumed other generations.

In Part IV, 'the faithful' we find songs for those who trust in a purpose for their lives – a purpose extending beyond their own needs, wants and desires to serve the greater good of life itself. That purpose could be one of a spiritual nature – a faith in a higher power or devotion to a being of supremacy. That purpose could be of a humanitarian nature – the desire to better the state of humans and their lives for personal, moral or logical reasons. That purpose may be of an unknown nature – where the drive of an individual's inner self unexplainably propels them towards positive social change, perhaps even in ways that seem contrary to the logic or traditions of others.

Within the songs 'for the faithful', readers will note re-occurring references to nature and maintaining balance between the spiritual, physical, ecological and social aspects of our lives. Though my faith is primarily inspired by the teachings of the Qur'an, there are subtleties within this section that draw from diverse oral and scriptural traditions throughout history. It is my hope that readers accept references to God and worship through prayer, meditation, fasting or pilgrimage as reflections of my faith perspective, and will simultaneously find peace within their own methods of engaging life's mystery and purpose.

Lastly, my offerings in Part V to 'the King's court' stand as messages – sometimes satirical and sometimes scathing – ringing out to the world's leaders on behalf of those who are all too often denied a voice or platform to speak for justice.

With regards to the book's contents, some readers may notice differences between the written versions of certain songs and their recorded counterparts which have appeared on albums I have recorded in the past. In an effort to draw more attention to the meanings of these writings as works of poetry, I have taken some phrases which, when sung, are often repeated to fill time or fit more smoothly to a metre, and have presented them only once. However where songs have reoccurring refrains that conceptually link several different verses together, I have not omitted any repeated text.

Some songs have also been adjusted to make their meanings more universally acceptable, particularly in cases where audience response to my original use of certain words indicated general misunderstandings of my work, requiring clarification. A good example of this may be found in a song like *Sing, Children of The World*. Originally, I wrote:

> Sing, children of the world,
> come together and hear the call.
> Sing, children of the world,
> *islam* will unite us all.

A song celebrating the equality of all humankind, as well as the innocence and purity of all children around the world, I chose to use the Arabic word *islam* to reflect how the concept of surrender to God, as our common creator, places us all on a playing field of equality with a goal of unity. Unfortunately my use of the word *islam* was interpreted by many as the proper name for an organized religion, insinuating that 'belonging' to a specific religious community is synonymous with 'unity'. With such logic, I shuddered at the implication that 'unity' may *not* be achieved if people were to belong to 'other' groups and thus, altered the phrase to read:

> Sing, children of the world,
> come together and hear the call.
> Sing, children of the world,
> *the truth* will unite us all.

Another example of a prominent change occurring in several songs (including *Al Khaliq* among others) is the absence of the word 'He' in reference to 'God' or 'Allah'. I have done this to more accurately represent my belief and understanding of The Creator as a being beyond the limitations of human gender.

A few explanations should be made about the textual layout of these writings. The capitalization of some words (or lack of capitalization in certain cases), the use of italics throughout the text and the use of Arabic phrases in some songs – all play a crucial role in the conceptual understanding of these poems, even those simple verses which may have initially been intended for the education or enjoyment of young children.

Proper names of people and places have been capitalized, including the words 'God' when used to refer to that singular 'being' turned to in worship or devotion. Similarly, the attributes of God are also capitalized, e.g. 'the Creator' or 'the Merciful', as are transliterated Arabic words, e.g. 'Allah', 'Makkah', 'Al Rahman' or 'Al Madinah'. However, a conscious effort has been made to avoid mischaracterizing certain words through inappropriate capitalization, whether in English or in transliterated Arabic form.

The word *islam*, for example, has come to be used by many English- and Arabic-speaking individuals as a noun, evolving into the capitalized proper name of a religion called 'Islam'. My approach, however, is to recognize the word *islam* as an Arabic gerund – the action of entering into peace through surrender to the will of the Creator. Thus the word does not appear in capitalized form throughout the book when transliterated, unless it appears at the beginning of a sentence. Similarly the word *muslim* is spelt without a capital 'M', due to my desire that its meaning (i.e., one who 'surrenders' to God or 'enters into peace' through willed surrender) remains its primary focus. As a writer, it is important for me to clarify these subtle semantics so that my works – and the philosophy which they are built upon – may be interpreted as I have intended.

Italics have often been used whenever a word or a phrase in a language other than English is used to convey an idea. Due to my fascination with, and immersion in, the Qur'an since my early twenties, many of these writings include phrases or words drawn from it – which was originally revealed and preserved in Arabic.

In most cases, Arabic words were used within these poems because they have no direct English equivalents, or it would have required several English words to accommodate an accurate translation of their meaning, e.g. *hijab, islam* or *salah*). Occasionally, however, I have adopted Arabic words or phrases in place of English words – drawing a direct correlation between the Qur'anic worldview and my work – for the sheer purposes of aesthetic preference (e.g. using 'Allah' instead of 'the God') or to help maintain the structure or metre of a specific song. An appendix at the end of this anthology contains my interpretations of any word or phrase from another language used throughout these writings.

For whom *does* the troubadour sing? For the travellers? The inspired or those who seek to find? For the faithful or the kings and their courts? 'A wise man's question, contains half the answer', said Solomon ibn Gabirol. So join me on this road and enjoy the journey. *Bismillah.*

Peace.
Dawud H. Wharnsby Ali
Denver, Colorado, USA,
December 2008

Acknowledgments

Though writing is an intimate process for me, in rare circumstances during my career, I have composed with close friends. Such collaborations were usually sparked by shared emotional experiences between myself and the individual (or individuals) writing with me, and not born out of a planned commercial effort to 'sit down and write a song together'.

In the case of co-written material contained within this collection (where complete lines, stanzas or words of a song were fully conceptualized by another person, then pieced together with my own words) a handful of people must be acknowledged.

My boyhood friend Bill Kocher takes direct co-writing credit on the songs *Love Strong*, *Argus Array*, *Gone* (*Yukon Sydney*), *Block*, *Dip in the Shallow End* and *Vacuous Waxing*. Zain Bhikha and Yusuf Islam – both tremendous inspirations and mentors to me – contributed lyrics and wrote an entire second verse for *The Prophet's Hands*. Asifa Sheikh and Jen Zaghloul built the primary foundation of *Ya Ummati*, and then granted me the privilege of lyrically embellishing their powerful song. *The Blue Sky is Blue* (*Like Blue Bubble Gum*) originated as a refrain composed and sung by my close friend Imran Al-Bakhkam when he was only four years old. The verses were assembled from words and wisdom I heard him express at various times between the ages of two and four.

There are certain songs within this collection which I wrote or co-wrote based on very specific suggestions from other artists, composers or producers. Peace activist and media developer Abdul Malik Mujahid outlined ideas which evolved into the songs *Wings Against My Window* and *Hi Neighbour, Salam Neighbour*. Several songs in Part I, 'To Inspire', were developed in consultation with Canadian film producer Abdul Rehman Michael Milo to accompany animated sequences produced for television. The Moroccan composer Mohamed Benammi developed the basic outline for what eventually became *Fi Qalbi* (*In My Heart*). Canadian-Chilean Zahra Duran assisted me in the development of *The Veil*. Syrian *nashid* singer Imad Rami presented me with a musical template that inspired my lyrics to *War/La ilaha illallah*. British composer and recording artist Sami Yusuf and I worked closely on the development of *What Has Become*, rooted deeply in his passion for the song's subject matter and built firmly against his original musical composition. Similarly, lyrics to *Eight Years Old* and *Let It Go* were written directly to correspond with musical arrangements by American composer and pianist Idris Phillips.

D.W.

Author's Notes on Terms and Phrases

'Alaihis salam – 'Upon him be peace.'

Al Fatiha – '*The Opening*', referring to the first chapter of the Qur'an.

Alhamdulillah – 'All praise is to God.'

Alhamdulillahir Rabbil 'alamin – 'All praise is to God, Lord of the Worlds.'

Al islam – See '*islam*'.

Al Khaliq – 'The Creator.'

Allah – 'The God.'

Allah Ta'ala – 'God Most High.'

Allahu ahad – 'God is One.'

Allahu akbar – 'God is Great.'

Allahumma salli 'ala Muhammad – 'Our God, place honour upon Muhammad.'

Al Madinah – 'The City', see also '*Al Madinatul Munawarah*.'

Al Madinatul Munawarah – 'The Enlightened City', referring to the city in Arabia once known as Yathrib. In 622 C.E., Muhammad migrated from his home in Makkah to Yathrib, shortly thereafter the city was re-named *Al Madinatul Munawarah* and to this day remains known as *Al Madinah*.

Anashid – Plural form of '*nashid*' meaning: a song of a spiritual, motivational or moral nature, traditionally sung a capella or presented with simple musical accompaniment, usually a single-sided hand-drum.

Ansar – 'Helpers', referring to those citizens of Yathrib (later called Madinah) who welcomed Muhammad and his Companions, helping them after their migration from the Arabian city of Makkah in 622 C.E.

Argus – Referring to 'Argus Panoptes' (The All Seeing), from Greek mythology. Argus is a mythological 'guardian' (with one hundred eyes), commanded to guard a sacred white heifer. ARGUS is the name given to a non-profit agency in Ontario, Canada, where young people between the ages 16 and 24 are offered a supportive living environment.

Ar Rahman – 'The Merciful.'

Ash hadu alla ilaha illallah wa ash hadu anna Muhammadur rasulullah – 'I testify that (there is) no god, except the God, and I testify that Muhammad is the messenger of God.'

'Asr – 'Declining day.' Referring to the late afternoon period when the sun has begun to decline towards the horizon. This marks the third period of the day in which the Qur'an encourages people to worship God.

As salamu 'alaikum – 'Peace be upon you.' A traditional Qur'anic greeting.

Azan – 'The Call', referring to the method given to gathering worshippers for congregational prayer.

Bismillah – 'In the name of the God'.

Bismillahir Rahmanir Rahim – 'In the name of the God, the Gracious, the Merciful.'

Fajr – 'The morning hours.' Referring to the dawn period when the sky lightens, but the sun has not yet risen over the horizon. This marks the first period of the day when the Qur'an encourages people to wake from sleep and worship God.

Fi qalbi – 'In my heart.'

Ful – Short for *ful medames, ful* is a dish made from cooked fava beans. It is commonly eaten in the Arab world as a morning meal on its own or with bread.

Hijab – 'to Conceal.' Used as a noun, it may refer to unspecific, modest, loose clothing that 'conceals'. It may also refer to a headscarf sometimes worn by women, in accordance with their interpretation of the Qur'an and the teachings of Muhammad.

Hijrah – 'Migration', referring to the migration of Muhammad and his Companions from the Arabian city of Makkah to Madinah in 622 C.E.

Hayya 'alal falah – 'Come quickly to success.'

Hayya 'alas salah – 'Come quickly to prayer.'

'Ibadah – 'Worship.'

I.C.E. – American English acronym for Immigration and Customs Enforcement, a division of the US Government's Homeland Security Department, monitoring all ports of entry in and out of the USA. Formerly known as the Immigration and Naturalization Services (I.N.S.).

Iftar – The evening meal, taken upon completion of one's daily fast.

Iman – 'Faith' or 'belief'.

Insha Allah – 'God willing.'

'Isha – Referring to the night period when the sun has fully declined over the horizon. *'Isha* marks the fifth period of a day's cycle when the Qur'an encourages people to worship God.

Islam – (or *Al islam*) The act of surrender, willful submission or entering into peace. From the Arabic root *s-l-m* (*salam*), meaning 'peace'.

Jihad – 'Struggle.'

Jalla jalaluhu – 'Majestic is the God.'

La ilaha illallah – '(There is) no god except the God.'

La ilaha ilallah, Muhammadur rasullulah – '(There is) no god except the God. Muhammad is the messenger of God.'

Madinah – 'City.' See also *Al Madinatul Munawarah*.

Madinatun Nabi – 'City of the Prophet'. See also *Al Madinatul Munawarah*.

Maghrib – 'West' or 'of the setting (sun)', referring to the early evening period when the sun has just declined over the horizon. *Maghrib* marks the fourth period of the day when the Qur'an encourages people to worship God.

Makkah – Ancient city of Arabia in which rests what many believe to be the first place of worship dedicated to 'the One God', established by the prophet Abraham. Makkah was also the birth place of Muhammad, a direct descendent of Abraham through Ishmael, in 570 C.E. Makkah remains a centre of spiritual and religious pilgrimage to this day.

Masjidun Nabi – 'The Prophet's place of prostration.' It refers also to the structure established in Madinah, Arabia, by

Muhammad and his Companions for the purpose of communal gathering, study, celebration and worship.

Muhammadur rasulullah – 'Muhammad is the messenger of God.'

Muslim – One who is engaged in acts of 'willful surrender' or 'willful submission' to God; the act of 'entering into peace'. As with the word *islam*, *muslim* also stems from the Arabic root *s-l-m* (*salam*), meaning 'peace'.

Qad qamatis salah – 'Come quickly to praise/prayer/worship.'

Qur'an – '(The) Recitation' or 'That which is to be recited', in reference to the collected recitations of Muhammad, described within as being a revelation from God.

Rabbana lakal hamd – 'Our Lord, for you is all praise.'

Ramadan – The ninth month of the lunar calendar. The Qur'an decrees this a 'sacred month' to be a period of worship and fasting for believers.

Ruku – 'Bowing', referring to the action of bowing at the waist as an act of worship to God.

Salam – 'Peace.'

Sallallahu 'alaihi wa sallam – 'Honour and peace upon him.'

Sami Allahu liman hamidah – 'God hears, for God is Praise.'

Shalom – The Hebrew word for 'peace', 'completeness' and 'welfare'.

Subhanallah walhamdulillah wa Allahu akbar – 'Glory be to God and praise be to God and God is great.'

Subhana Rabbiyal a'la – 'Glory to the Lord, Most High.'

Subhana Rabbiyal 'azim – 'Glory to the Lord, Most Elevated.'

Suhur – A light, pre-dawn meal, taken prior to a day of fasting, usually in the month of Ramadan.

Ummah – 'Nation (of people).'

Ummati – 'My nation (of people).'

Wa 'alaikum as salam – 'And upon you, peace'. Response to the greeting of *As salamu 'alaikum*.

Wudu – Ablutions prescribed in the Qur'an (the washing of the face, arms, and feet to the ankles and the wiping of the head) to be done as a means of purification in preparation for prayer.

Ya Allah – 'Oh God.'

Ya Ghafur – 'Oh The Forgiver.'

Ya Rabbal 'alameen – 'Oh, Lord of The Worlds.'

Ya Rahman – 'Oh Merciful.'

Ya Subhanahu wa ta'ala – 'Oh glory to God, the Most High.'

Yathrib – An oasis city in Arabia, dating back to the sixth century B.C.E., now known as *Al Madinatul Munawarah*. See also *Al Madinatul Munawarah*.

Ya Ummati – 'Oh, my nation (of people).'

Zikr – 'Remembrance (of God).'